CALL IT A DAY

A Comedy in Three Acts

BY

DODIE SMITH
(C. L. ANTHONY)

Copyright, 1935, by D. G. Smith
Copyright, 1936, by D. G. Smith
Copyright (Acting Edition), 1937, by D. G. Smith

All rights reserved

SAMUEL FRENCH, LTD.
26 Southampton Street, Strand, London, W.C.2
SAMUEL FRENCH, INC.
25 West 45th Street, New York, U.S.A.
7623 Sunset Boulevard, Hollywood 46, Cal.
SAMUEL FRENCH (CANADA), LTD.
480 University Avenue, Toronto

Copyright © 1935 by D.G. Smith
Copyright © 1936 by D.G. Smith
All Rights Reserved

CALL IT A DAY is fully protected under the copyright laws of the British Commonwealth, including Canada, the United States of America, and all other countries of the Copyright Union. All rights, including professional and amateur stage productions, recitation, lecturing, public reading, motion picture, radio broadcasting, television and the rights of translation into foreign languages are strictly reserved.

ISBN 978-0-573-11242-3

www.samuelfrench.co.uk
www.samuelfrench.com

For Amateur Production Enquiries

United Kingdom and World excluding North America

plays@SamuelFrench-London.co.uk
020 7255 4302/01

Each title is subject to availability from Samuel French, depending upon country of performance.

CAUTION: Professional and amateur producers are hereby warned that CALL IT A DAY is subject to a licensing fee. Publication of this play does not imply availability for performance. Both amateurs and professionals considering a production are strongly advised to apply to the appropriate agent before starting rehearsals, advertising, or booking a theatre. A licensing fee must be paid whether the title is presented for charity or gain and whether or not admission is charged.

The professional rights in this play are controlled by Film Rights Ltd in association with Laurence Fitch Ltd, 11 Pandora Road, London NW6 1TS.

No one shall make any changes in this title for the purpose of production. No part of this book may be reproduced, stored in a retrieval system, or transmitted in any form, by any means, now known or yet to be invented, including mechanical, electronic, photocopying, recording, videotaping, or otherwise, without the prior written permission of the publisher. No one shall upload this title, or part of this title, to any social media websites.

The right of Dodie Smith to be identified as author of this work has been asserted in accordance with Section 77 of the Copyright, Designs and Patents Act 1988.

CALL IT A DAY

Produced at the Globe Theatre, Shaftesbury Avenue, London, W.1, on October 30th, 1935, with the following cast of characters:

(In the order of their appearance)

DOROTHY HILTON	*Fay Compton.*
ROGER HILTON	*Owen Nares.*
VERA	*Mavis Clair.*
ANN HILTON	*Alexis France.*
MARTIN HILTON	*Geoffrey Nares.*
CATHERINE HILTON	*Patricia Hilliard.*
COOK	*Muriel George.*
MRS. MILSOM	*Phyllis Morris.*
PAUL FRANCIS	*Austin Trevor.*
ETHEL FRANCIS	*Lois Heatherley.*
MURIEL WESTON	*Marie Löhr.*
FRANK HAINES	*George Thorpe.*
ELSIE LESTER	*Ann Wilton.*
BEATRICE GWYNNE	*Valerie Taylor.*
ALISTAIR BROWN	*Bryan Coleman.*
JOAN COLLETT	*Moira Reed.*

The Play Produced by BASIL DEAN.

SYNOPSIS OF SCENES

ACT I

Scene 1.—Roger and Dorothy Hilton's bedroom in their house in St. John's Wood. 8 a.m.
Scene 2.—The Kitchen. 8.30 a.m.
Scene 3.—The Dining-room. 8.55 a.m.

ACT II

Scene 1.—Paul Francis's Studio in Holland Park. 4.45 p.m.
Scene 2.—Frank Haines's Flat in Jermyn Street. 5.15 p.m.
Scene 3.—Roger Hilton's Office in Gray's Inn. 5.55 p.m.

ACT III

Scene 1.—The Back Garden of the Hilton's House. 6.45 p.m.
Scene 2.—Ann and Catherine Hilton's Bedroom. 11.30 p.m.
Scene 3.—Roger and Dorothy Hilton's Bedroom. 11.45 p.m.

The action of the play takes place between 8 a.m. and midnight of a day in early spring.

CALL IT A DAY

(SUGGESTIONS FOR AMATEURS)

CALL IT A DAY

This play, while being admirably adapted for the use of Amateur Dramatic Societies as regards subject, parts, etc., presents certain difficulties regarding settings and furniture. These difficulties may, at first sight, seem unsurmountable, but a careful study of the suggestions given here will, it is hoped, place the play within the scope of the majority. Naturally all suggestions must be altered to suit the requirements of individual societies, many of which may be fórtunate enough to possess producers capable of thinking out alternative schemes or improving on the ones suggested; but they will be a helpful basis.

The play is in nine scenes and requires eight different sets. It should be possible for amateurs to play it in two simple interior sets, effecting the changes by different curtains, furniture and disguising of doors and windows (this will *not* cover the Garden Scene, which will be dealt with separately). The furniture, which presents, on first sight, a formidable problem, can be cut down by clever management to very little more than is required for one really well-furnished set, and certainly not more than is needed by the average play with two full interiors.

Positions of doors, furniture, etc., have been kept as near as possible to those in the London production, so that the movements of characters can be followed as printed. Occasionally these will have to be altered to suit the simplified sets, but very simple stage management will arrange for this.

The permanent set for Act I should be as follows:

Walls painted some pleasant neutral colour such as beige or yellow, which might be found in a bedroom, a kitchen or a dining-room of a St. John's Wood house. Door centre of right wall, another in left of back wall, another in right of back wall—a comfortable space for two beds and bedside table between these doors. A casement window in left wall (see Plan 1).

Scene 1.—*Roger and Dorothy's Bedroom.* (See Plan 2.)

The door on right is supposed to lead to the passage, the door right of back wall to Roger's dressing-room, that on left to the bathroom. These doors should not be widely opened as it is very difficult to make the backing look convincing.

The window now has pleasant chintz curtains.

Furniture.

Twin beds in centre of back wall, with bedside table between them. Dressing-table left with small stool.

No other furniture is required by the action, but may, of course, be used if there is room and time to set it.

Note.—The dressing-table should be chintz covered, and it would be

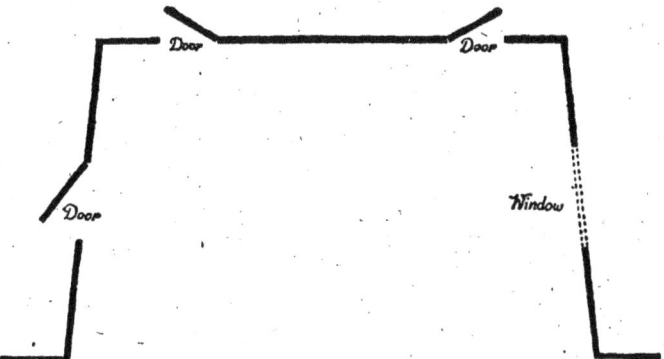

PLAN 1.—Set for Act I, Scenes 1, 2 and 3, and for Act III, Scenes 2 and 3
Set painted beige, yellow or cream
It will be found more convenient if all the doors open off

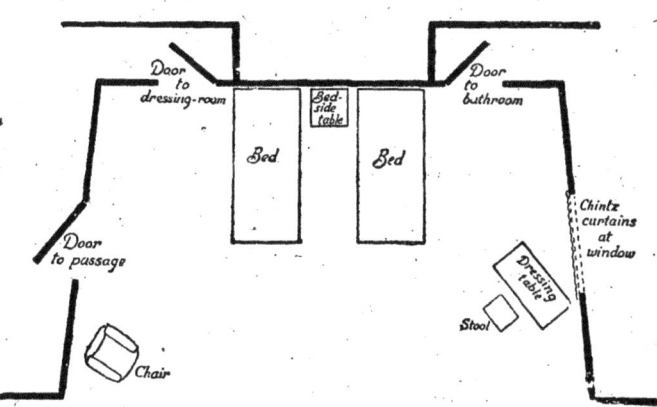

PLAN 2.—Set arranged for Act I, Scene 1, and Act III, Scene 3

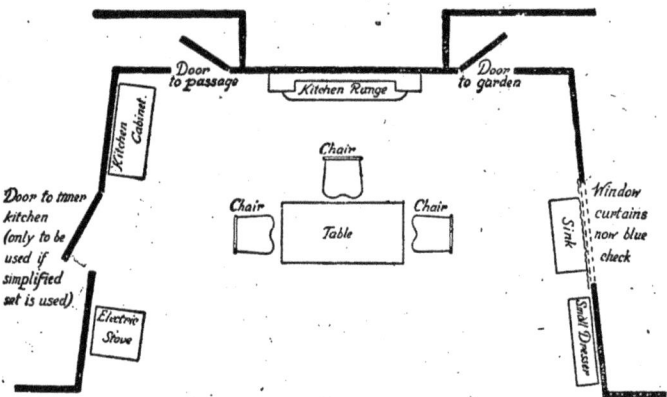

PLAN 3.—Set arranged for Act I, Scene 2
For simplified arrangement the same, but without stove, dresser and range

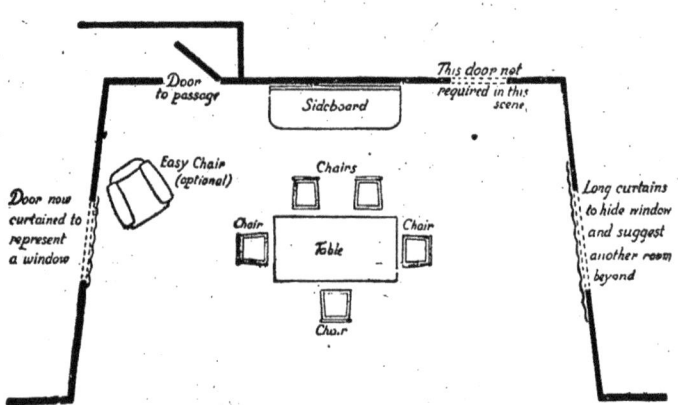

PLAN 4.—Set arranged for Act I, Scene 3

quite practicable to use the desk which is required for Act II, Scenes 2 and 3, with a loose frilled cover of chintz over it. If so it will not be practicable to open a drawer, and Dorothy's handkerchiefs must be kept in a chintz-covered box on the dressing-table.

SCENE 2.—*The Kitchen.* (See Plan 3.)

With the exception of the Garden Scene, this is the most difficult set in the play. Two schemes are given for it. The first is, as near as possible, similar to the set used in London and, therefore, far the best, as the audience likes to see plenty of detail in this type of scene. The second scheme is a simplification, which will require some alteration of the business as at present shown.

Scheme 1.

The door on right is not required, but can be presumed to lead to a pantry or larder.

The door right of back wall leads to the rest of the house. The door left of back wall leads to the garden (again, it should never be opened wide).

The window has short blue check curtains. (All these changeable curtains should be ready on rods and simply put up on brackets when the scene is changed).

Furniture.

Kitchen table centre with three chairs, electric stove below door in right wall (electric stoves are easier to fake than gas stoves). Kitchen cabinet above this door. Kitchen range in centre of back wall. Sink in front of window, small dresser below window in left wall; this alters position of dresser from original production, but only changes Vera's movements very slightly. Dustbin below sink. Picture of cows over mantelpiece. Canisters, crockery, trays, etc., as required.

As will be seen, this is a very heavy list of heavy pieces of furniture, but certain simplifications can be made without spoiling the business. The dresser is only used when Vera gets the slop-basin from it; it can be left out—it is a most difficult piece to move with all its crockery—and Vera can have left the slop-basin on the kitchen table. The canisters in the kitchen cabinet are absolutely necessary, but they could be on a small hanging shelf or in a small light cupboard.

The kitchen range should be a stage " prop," quite light to carry on and off—the electric stove also, as a real one is very heavy.

The sink—the taps do not have to be practicable—is not a serious problem. It can be very small and on a stand, or even a box with a curtain round it, and the dustbin to one side.

Scheme 2. (Same as Plan 3 but minus range, stove and dresser.)

In this simplified plan the door in right wall should be used and presumed to lead to an inner kitchen where the cooking is done. Thus only kitchen table and chairs, small sink and some form of kitchen cabinet or cupboard are required. This will necessitate some alterations in business. Thus, Vera is off stage doing the toast and stands at the door to talk to Cook. Cook must be on stage, so she cannot be at the range at the opening of the scene; she must find some other business, such as getting the breakfast-tray ready. Later she will take the teapot *off* to make the tea and bring the bacon back from the other kitchen. Neat timing of movements will make these small changes quite practicable. If absolutely necessary, the sink can also be banished to the inner kitchen, but this makes the business at the curtain of the play very tricky as Cook would have to break the plate off stage. It has been found that the audience do not laugh until they actually see the broken pieces (which should be in the sink in case the plate does not break). If the breakage has to occur off stage Cook must re-enter with the broken pieces in her hand, open the back-door and throw them into a dustbin just outside. This will need careful timing or the curtain laugh will be spoilt.

If this simplified scheme is used. care must be taken that the room does not look too much like a sitting-room. Touches to suggest a kitchen can be thought out to replace range and stove, etc.—a long brush, perhaps a saucepan rack—anything small and easily carried on which will give atmosphere. If the range and mantelshelf is off stage there must be a table in its place for the clock, etc.

Naturally Scheme 1 is better than Scheme 2, but it presents real difficulties. Probably the best solution is a compromise between the two, such as putting the stove off stage and the range on, simplifying the kitchen cabinet and replacing the dresser by a table—or simply using the drainer of the sink. But obviously as much detail as possible should be included, as a kitchen scene is always rather a novelty and very pleasing to the audience.

SCENE 3.—*Dining-room.* (See Plan 4.)

The door, which should open outwards in right wall, is now turned into a window by the addition of long curtains. It should be filled in for a couple of feet at the bottom by a small piece of wood painted to match the walls. Some producers will no doubt find that they are able to make this change more realistic if the door in the right wall of the main set (see Plan 1) is hinged downstage.

The door right of back wall leads to the passage. The door left of back wall is not required. It can either be ignored or hidden by a bookcase and picture. The window is now completely hidden by long heavy curtains which suggest they have taken the place of double doors.

It is, of course, just as practicable to place these heavy curtains over the door right and to continue to treat the window as a window, but the method suggested will make the scene look much fresher and will enable the movements of the characters to be kept as at present.

Furniture.

All that is absolutely essential is: the dining-table and five small chairs (the kitchen table may remain on, disguised by a large and pretty breakfast-cloth). It will, however, be an advantage to have a small sideboard at the centre back and a small table for the clock—or the clock may stand on the sideboard. It is immaterial where the clock is provided it is on somewhere.

It is *not* necessary to have the fireplace and gas-stove as there is no business connected with them. Ann mentions the gas-stove in Act III, but it can be presumed to be in the fourth wall.

Vera is supposed to kneel in an armchair by the window, but she can quite well stand up to look out. But as two armchairs are required later, one of them might as well make an appearance here, in a loose cover.

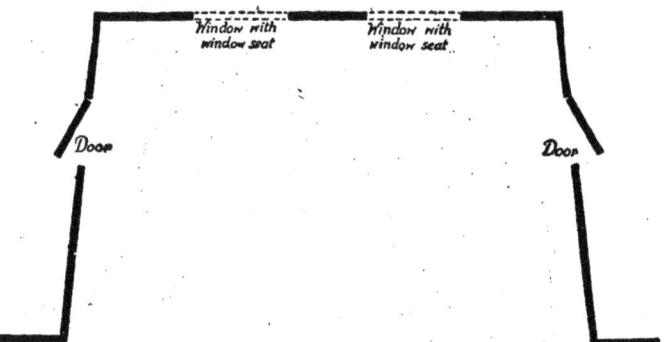

PLAN 5.—Set for Act II, Scenes 1, 2 and 3
Walls painted a rather pale olive green

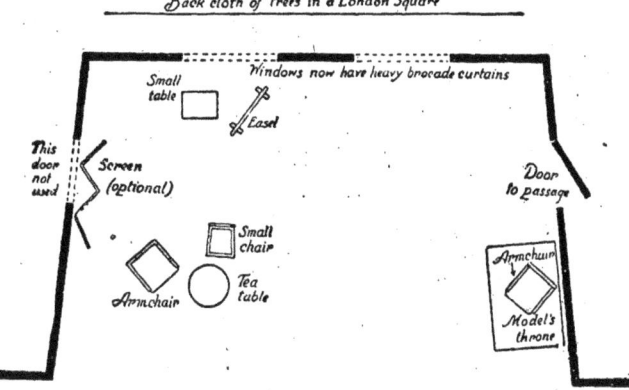

PLAN 6.—Set arranged for Act II, Scene 1

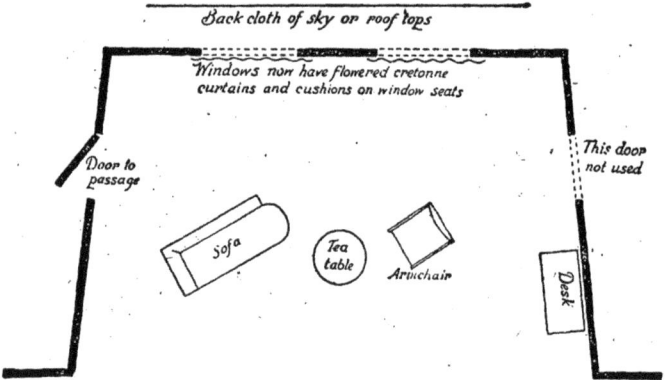

PLAN 7.—Set arranged for Act II, Scene 2

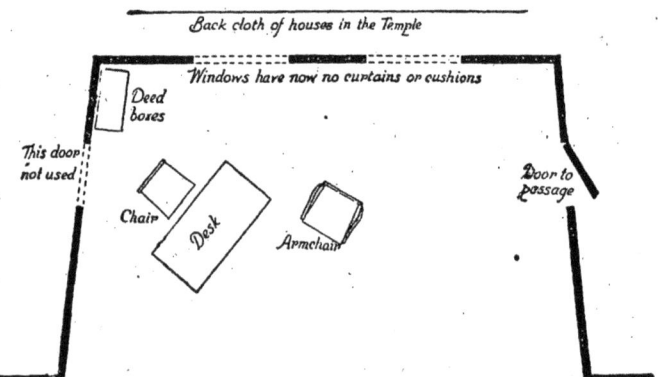

PLAN 8.—Set arranged for Act II, Scene 3

CALL IT A DAY. 13

This scene should be made to look lived-in and very pleasant, with one or two good pictures.

GENERAL NOTE ON ACT

All hangings, etc., should be chosen to make definite and contrasting colour schemes in each scene. Thus, if beige is chosen for the walls, the bedroom might have chintz or cretonne curtains of a floral design in which pink predominates; the kitchen curtains should be blue check; and the dining-room should have substantial curtains and hangings of, say, green or brown.

ACT II

Permanent set (see Plan 5).

Walls painted a rather pale but not unpleasant green, which would be suitable for all three sets.

Doors in centre of right and left walls.

Two good-sized sash windows, with window-seats and shutters, in back wall.

Note.—The action requires only one door in each set, but the presence of two will enable the entrance to be changed over in each scene, and whilst helping to change the appearance of the set, make it possible to retain most of the original movements.

SCENE 1. *Paul's Studio.* (See Plan 6.)

Door on left used for entrance.

Furniture.

Essential: Easel and small table up by right window, small armchair down right with fireside table (the same armchair as in Act I, but with different loose cover), stool or chair on model's throne left (a large flat box would pass as the throne if necessary, or it could be cut out entirely). Shelves with books, vases, etc. (on which stands the very small Rossetti sketch). Pictures, some old, some modern.

Every attempt should be made to give this scene atmosphere. The curtains should be heavy, old-fashioned brocade. There should be books and canvases stacked on the floor and the window-seats. A screen in front of the unwanted door would be a help. There should be a backcloth showing the trees in a London square.

SCENE 2.—*Frank Haines's Room in Jermyn Street.* (See Plan 7.)

Right door now used. The one on left can be ignored and presumed to lead to Frank's bedroom.

The windows should now have cretonne or rep curtains of a very conventional type. There should be a few cushions on the window-seats.

Furniture.

A sofa right centre, a small tea-table centre, an armchair left centre, a desk either between window or against left wall. (There will probably not be room for it between the windows and it will be more furnishing on the left wall.)

Note.—The sofa should be the type with only one end and a back. It would be quite practicable to use one of the beds, from Act I, with cushions and a loose cover—but if it has a head-board, it would have to be removed and then replaced for Act III.

The tea-table should be the one used in the previous Studio scene, with an afternoon teacloth (no cloth in Studio scene).

The armchair should be the one used in the Studio scene, but either with a different loose cover or, if it is leather, with no cover.

The desk should have made its appearance already as a dressing-table, with chintz cover, in Act I.

A few conventional pictures in marked contrast to those in the Studio will help this scene.

There should be a backcloth of sky or house-tops.

SCENE 3.—*Roger Hilton's Office.* (See Plan 8.)

Left door now used. The right door ignored. The windows should now be without curtains or cushions.

Furniture.

A desk right centre. Two chairs, one behind it, one facing it. A few deed-boxes, on a shelf or standing on top of each other. Other office furniture, such as a filing cabinet, may be used, but is not at all essential.

Note.—The desk should be the one used in the previous scene, when the side and front of it will have been seen. We shall now see the back and, with a house telephone and official-looking folders, etc., on it, it will look sufficiently different.

The chairs can have been used in the dining-room in Act I (preferably they should have arms).

No pictures in this scene except a framed certificate.

ACT III

Scene 1—The Garden—will be dealt with later.

Scenes 2 and 3 require the permanent set as in Act I.

SCENE 2.—*Catherine and Ann Hilton's Bedroom.* (See Plan 9.)

Preferably the door in right wall should be turned into a window (as suggested in Act I, Scene 3). The door in right of back wall should be ignored or covered by curtain, the door in left of back wall used as the entrance, and the window left should be hidden by a small wardrobe, bookshelf or curtain.

Furniture.

Bed extreme right corner of back wall, running parallel with this wall. Bed left centre running downwards from back wall. Small bookcase near this bed ; two small bedside tables with lamps.

Note.—It is not absolutely essential to have these tables or lamps or to put on the light at all. It may be better to play the entire scene by moonlight as it will reveal it less to the audience.

The above arrangement will enable the actors to use the original positions and movements, but it would be quite simple to reverse them all, using left as right, in which case the original window in the left wall can be used (see Plan 10).

Note.—The same beds should be used as in the parents' bedroom, which follows immediately after, but they should have different coloured eiderdowns. It will help the effect of moonlight if these are blue and the window curtains white muslin. Very little is seen of the detail in this scene, but there should be a few careful touches to differentiate it from the parents' bedroom. The pictures over Ann's bed will help. These

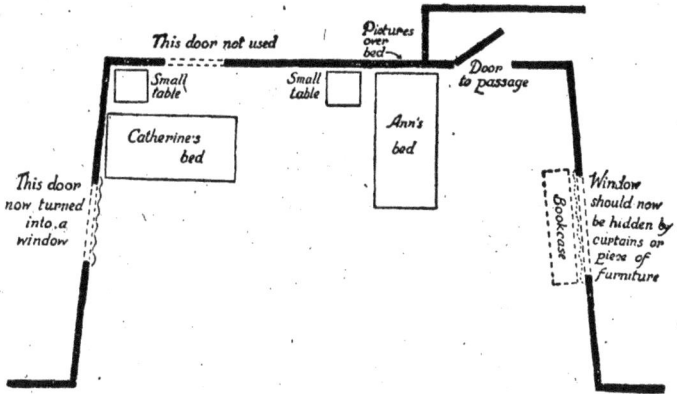

PLAN 9.—Set arranged for Act III, Scene 2

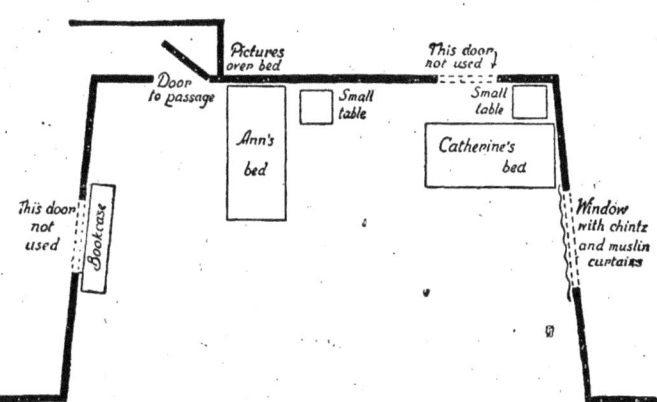

PLAN 10.—Alternative arrangement for Act III, Scene 2

Note.—In this arrangement it might be better to use the door **in** the R. wall and put the bookcase across the one R. of back wall.

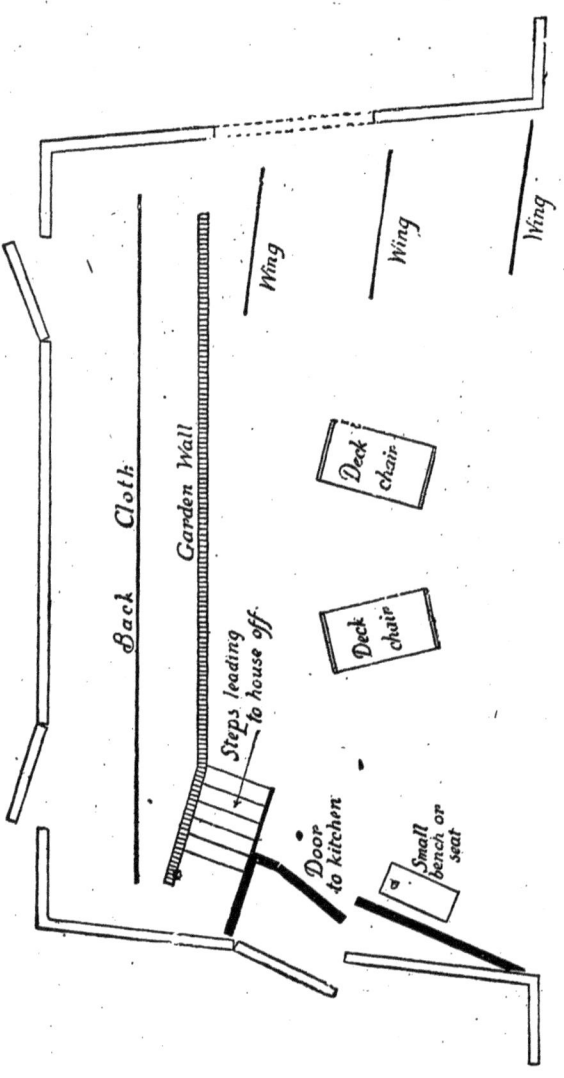

PLAN II.—Simplified arrangement of Garden Scene. Act III, Scene 1

This is set inside the interior set, which is thus ready for Scene 2. Interior set, ready for Scene 2, shown by spaced lines.

This arrangement presumes it is possible to fly the small flat on R. If not, the R. wall of interior set cannot be completely set till after the flat has been moved.

Note the extreme simplification of this set. All it requires is:

Back cloth. Wall (which could be built in sections). Three garden wings. A few steps to lead off. Very small flat with door to kitchen. Two deck-chairs. One bench or chair.

will be rather troublesome to hang quickly unless some clever method is thought out. They might be ready hung on a board painted to match the walls, which could be quickly placed in position—in the dim light the board would hardly show. Or they might be unframed and put up either with drawing pins or with adhesive paper.

It will be found essential that Catherine's bed should run parallel to the audience and not up and down stage, so that the two girls can be seen clearly during their scene on it.

SCENE 3.—*Roger and Dorothy's Bedroom*

As in Act I, Scene 1, but at night. The beds from previous scene will be placed in their correct positions with their original eiderdowns. The correct window curtains will be hung, dressing-table brought on and Ann's pictures and bookcase removed.

THE GARDEN SCENE. *Act III, Scene 1.*

It is necessary to deal with this scene separately, because it does not fit in with either of the two suggested sets and each society will have to invent their own method of managing it. The ideal way is as follows:

To have a separate set built, as like the original London production as possible, probably simplifying the elaborate backings with a well-painted back cloth. As the scene follows the interval there would be plenty of time to set it and, as it is the longest scene in the play, the audience will not mind a reasonable wait while it is struck and the children's bedroom is set, particularly if the other changes have been swift.

Many wealthy societies who play on a good-sized stage may be able to follow the above method, or a simplification of it. In smaller societies the following suggestions are given (see Plan 11):

During the interval, place the permanent set for Acts I and III in position, ready for the last two scenes. Then hang a painted backcloth, or even a grey curtain, inside the whole back wall. In front of this put a small property wall; if it is not practicable to sit on this wall Joan must first stand the other side of it while she talks and Martin must get her a box to climb over it so that she never has to put her weight on it. (In London she *returned* by climbing over near the balcony steps, which simplified her exit.)

On the left of the stage, place some wings, painted with trees and greenery.

On the right, place a flat representing the wall of the house. Naturally it is better if this can have kitchen door and steps up to the balcony, but it would be quite practicable to have *only* the kitchen door fully seen and the entrance to the house up-stage between the flat and the back cloth—in which case a few steps would help the illusion that people were going off up some stairs to a back door or balcony.

This method of arrangement presumes that it is possible to fly the small flat on the right. If not, the right wall of the interior set cannot be completely set until after the Garden Scene has been struck. The lighting of the whole scene should be very dim—which will not only cover up a multitude of evils, but help the atmosphere.

The only furniture required for this scene is two deck-chairs and a bench or chair for the Cook.

The whole scene is of the utmost importance to the play and will repay any trouble taken over it. A little illusion—ivy, a few shrubs, the suggestion of the backs of houses on the backcloth—will go a long way. It is not really as difficult as it looks.

GENERAL NOTES

It has been shown that the actual amount of scenery need not be very much and that, by clever management, the furniture can be considerably cut down. It will, however, require very careful thought if the scenes are really to appear different. Hangings, curtains, loose-covers, table-cloths, etc., must be sharply differentiated, and many producers may be able to think of their own little touches to alter the appearances of sets.

One very important point is that the changes should be made speedily, and this will call for much planning and rehearsal. Here are a few suggestions that may help:

In every case, scenes possess two entrances (the set for Act I has three). Thus furniture can be taken *off* through one door and brought *on* through another, so avoiding collisions. While it is being taken on and off, one person can be hanging curtains and changing loose-covers and pictures. On small stages it is very difficult to have too many people about, and it might be practicable to give some of the cast definite jobs to do at the close of each scene. It is not advisable to worry players who are just going to appear in a scene and they should keep off stage till it is set. But the players who have *completed* their scene might easily help. As an example:

After the Studio scene (Act II, Scene 1)—
The actress playing Ethel Francis might be responsible for—
(1) Removing the loose cover from her chair and leaving it ready for Scene 2.
(2) Taking her tea-tray off stage.
The actor playing Paul might—
(1) Remove his own easel.
(2) Take down and remove his pictures.
Both going off at right door while sofa, etc., is coming on at left door.

Note.—Probably only those players who are actually on stage at the curtain of each scene should help. Unless very well rehearsed it will cause confusion if those who have made their exits run back again.

If very well planned, the changes should be extremely effective and very swift, but they must be rehearsed as carefully as the actual play.

Finally, " Call it a Day " is a play of detail—detail of story, detail of character drawing, detail of family life. Detail is responsible for much of its success. But, though it is elaborate, it is not extravagant, and should be practicable for any society who will make ingenuity take the place of elaboration. It is a play that gives particularly good scope to women—there are eleven good women's parts. It will probably be found practicable to enroll many of these ladies as helpers as regards curtains, kitchen fittings, etc. It is a play in which women can be of enormous help in every way.

CALL IT A DAY

ACT I

SCENE 1

SCENE.—DOROTHY and ROGER HILTON'S *bedroom in their house in St. John's Wood. A day in spring.* 8 a.m.
The entrance from a landing is in the wall R. *Up* R., *in the back wall, is a door leading into* ROGER'S *dressing-room, and another door up* L. *leads to the bathroom. Between these doors are twin beds. The dressing-table is by the windows* L. *Bedside table and various small pieces of furniture as needed.*

The decorations and furniture are in good taste, but it is the taste of people who have been married twenty years ; the dressing-table looks like a dressing-table and carries a load of silver brushes and glass bottles. The window curtains are chintz, the electric light shades pink silk. The general colour of the room is pink and cream ; on the whole a pleasant if over-pretty room. Narrow shafts of sunlight have forced their way through the drawn curtains.

(*See Photograph of Scene.*)

When the CURTAIN *rises,* DOROTHY *and* ROGER HILTON *are asleep in the twin beds ;* ROGER, *in the right-hand bed, represented by a mound of clothes and a dishevelled lock of hair,* DOROTHY *lying with unruffled bedclothes and wearing a net bonnet to keep her wave in place, which is very becoming. The full light of day will reveal her as a little over forty, but the drawn curtains are kind and she has the gift of sleeping prettily—there is something a little childlike in the gentle relaxing of her features.*

For a moment DOROTHY *and* ROGER *sleep in peace. A church clock strikes eight. Then there is a knock at the door* R. DOROTHY *stirs.*

DOROTHY. Come in.

(VERA, *a pleasant-looking young maid in a fresh print dress, enters with a tray of morning tea and* "*The Times.*")

VERA (*crossing up between the beds*). Good morning, madam.
DOROTHY. Good morning, Vera.
VERA (*placing the tray on the table between the beds*). Shall I pour it for you, madam ?

DOROTHY. No, thank you. (*She yawns—but neatly—then sits up.*) Draw the curtains back, will you?

VERA (*crossing* L.). It's a lovely day, madam.

(*She draws the curtains back and the room is flooded with sunlight.*)

DOROTHY. Good gracious—it's quite dazzling.

VERA. It's the first real spring morning we've had.

DOROTHY. I expect it's pretty cold, though. (*She puts on the bedjacket.*)

VERA (*taking* DOROTHY'S *dressing-gown from the dressing-table stool to the bed*). No, madam, the air's quite soft. I went out without my coat—to take the little dog out.

DOROTHY. Do you like dogs, Vera? (*She begins to pour out the tea.*)

VERA (L. *of the bed*). Love them, madam—though I've never been with a terrier before. He was ever so frisky. It is nice up here, madam.

DOROTHY. Is this the first time you've worked in St. John's Wood?

VERA. Yes, madam. It's ever so pretty, with all the trees coming out.

DOROTHY. I hope you're going to like it.

VERA. Shall I put the bath on, madam?

DOROTHY. No, not just yet. Roger—wake up.—You'd better shake him, Vera.

VERA. Really, madam?

DOROTHY. Yes, really.

(VERA *crosses to* R. *of* ROGER'S *bed.*)

Someone always has to, and I hate getting out of bed to do it. Susan was a great shaker.

(VERA *shakes him gingerly.*)

Oh, much harder than that; you should have seen Susan.

(*Thus encouraged,* VERA *lets fly.* ROGER *gives a grunt of protest and huddles deeper into the bedclothes.* VERA *warms to her task.* ROGER *at last opens his eyes and looks at her. He is a pleasant-looking man, in the early forties.*)

ROGER (*still heavy with sleep*). Hello—who are you?

VERA. Vera, sir. I'm new.

(ROGER *gives a sleepy grunt of laughter.*)

I hope I didn't shake too hard.

ROGER. No—but you've a different technique from Susan—short and sharp instead of slow and steady.

VERA. I'll try to be steadier to-morrow, sir.

(ROGER *grunts and slips under the bedclothes again.*)

DOROTHY. He mustn't lie down again—he'll only be annoyed later.

(VERA *shakes him again.*)

ROGER. All right—all right, I'm awake.

DOROTHY. He's not really safe till he's had his tea. Put the bath on, Vera.

(VERA *crosses* L. *and goes into the bathroom.*)

Come on, Roger, tea's going cold. (*She hands him a cup.*)

(ROGER *runs through a distinguished repertoire of waking-up noises before taking the cup of tea. Finally, he sits stirring it, looking after* VERA.)

ROGER. I must say, Dot, I think you ought to shake me yourself.

DOROTHY. Certainly not. It gives me a headache. You always let Susan shake you.

ROGER. We'd had Susan donkey's years. It's very disconcerting to have strange females dashing at one in the early morning. And probably the girl doesn't like doing it.

(VERA *comes in from the bathroom and crosses* R.)

DOROTHY. Nonsense. You don't mind shaking the master, do you, Vera?

VERA (*stopping* R. *of* ROGER'S *bed*). Not at all, madam—provided there's no ill feeling.

DOROTHY. Splendid. Thank you, Vera.

(VERA *goes off through door* R.)

Quite a nice little thing, I think.

ROGER (*gloomily*). Very bright and chatty.

DOROTHY. I like people to be bright in the morning.

ROGER. I know you do, darling. You and Vera will be singing glees together. (*He looks at the window.*) Good Lord, look at that sun.

DOROTHY. I know. Vera says it's quite warm.

ROGER (*getting out of bed, at* L. *side*). Now I wonder why no one has the sense to wake me up an hour earlier on a morning like this? (*He puts on his slippers, which are on the floor just* L. *of his bed, and crosses to the dressing-table.*) I could have had an hour's run in the Park with Terry. It would have done the little beggar good.

DOROTHY. It wouldn't have done you any harm. You're putting on weight.

ROGER (*looking at himself in the glass*). This damn coat's shrunk.

DOROTHY. So have all your coats, I suppose.

ROGER. Now, look here—I can prove to you——

DOROTHY. You prove it to the bathroom scales.
ROGER. Certainly. I frequently consult the scales. (*He goes to the window and opens it with too much energy.*) Hell, there's that wretched next-door cat on our bulbs again. (*Shouting out of the window.*) Get off, you brute.
DOROTHY. Roger, do stop shouting.
ROGER. Ha—Terry's after her—good dog, fetch her out.
DOROTHY. Roger, be quiet.
ROGER. He's routed her—she's off like a streak of lightning. Good man there—worry her, lad.
DOROTHY. Roger, really! Those next-door people will think they've come to live amongst hooligans.
ROGER (*crossing* R.). I'm not going to curb a dog's natural instincts. (*He picks up his dressing-gown from the armchair down* R.)
DOROTHY. And what about the cat's natural instincts to go on our bulbs?
ROGER (*crossing to* L. *of* DOROTHY's *bed, putting on his dressing-gown*). That cat's natural instincts can be perfectly well satisfied in its own back garden.
DOROTHY. Oh, go to your bath—and don't forget the scales.
ROGER (L. *of* DOROTHY's *bed*). You know, you women with this skinny complex are laying up a wretched old age for yourselves. Stringy, that's what you'll be. Stringy and desiccated.
DOROTHY. Well, that's better than having two double chins and three double stomachs.
ROGER (*hitting his stomach*). I have no stomach whatever.
DOROTHY. How inconvenient.
ROGER. Now, look here, Dot, I'm serious. You ought to watch yourself. You're getting to an age when if a woman gets thin she stays thin.
 (*He exits into the bathroom.*)
DOROTHY. Thanks.

(*With* ROGER'S *remarks about skinniness in her mind,* DOROTHY *puts down her tea-cup and picks up a hand mirror from the bedside table. She examines her neck and appears to be slightly dissatisfied with it. Then she puts on horn-rimmed spectacles and prepares to read the paper. There is a knock at the door* R.)

Yes?

(ANN HILTON *enters, in a blue Jaeger dressing-gown. She is fifteen, with a highly intelligent little face.*)

ANN (*crossing to between the beds*). I say, Mum, I do think you might speak to Cath—she's bagged the bathroom first again.
DOROTHY. That really is rather selfish of her. Good morning, darling.
 (*They kiss.*)

Have you asked her how long she'll be? (*She takes the spectacles off.*)

ANN. Another ten minutes, she says, but you know what that means.

DOROTHY. I wonder if she'll hear if I shout. Open the door. (ANN *crosses to the door* R. *and opens it.*) (*Calling.*) Catherine, hurry up there. You'll make Ann late for school.

ANN. She's got the tap full on. (*She closes the door again and crosses to the bed.*) Oh dear, and I did want to be extra early this morning. I'm sure I've got one of the algebra questions down wrong. (*She sits on the* R. *side of* DOROTHY'S *bed.*) Mum—can you think of any possible use algebra can be in one's after-life?

DOROTHY. After-life?

ANN. I mean, after school life.

DOROTHY. Well, let me see now. (*After a pause.*) Of course, it must be some use or schools wouldn't teach it.

ANN. Wouldn't they just!

DOROTHY (*at last*). It helps your powers of reasoning.

ANN. It doesn't help mine. After I've done half an hour's algebra my brain feels most peculiar—sort of floating. Are you keen on having a daughter with a floating brain?

DOROTHY. Now, Ann—I am *not* going to get you off algebra. I got you off science——

ANN. But it's only so that I can spend more time on really important things—like poetry——

DOROTHY. And what good's poetry going to be to you in your after-life? It won't help you to look after a husband and children.

ANN. I'm not going to have a husband.

DOROTHY. You certainly aren't if something isn't done about that tooth of yours. Come here. (*She takes* ANN'S *head in her hands.*) Now smile—close your teeth. There, I thought so. I told Jordan he was taking that plate off too soon. You'll never get a husband if your teeth protrude.

ANN. I don't want a husband—and, anyhow, women with out-of-door teeth always get married. I expect it's because men are so fond of horses.

DOROTHY (*laughing*). Well, no one could like *one* out-of-door tooth. You must go to Mr. Jordan on Saturday morning.

ANN (*with a wail*). Oh, Mummy! I'm going to the Tate on Saturday morning.

DOROTHY. But you've been to the Tate lots of times.

ANN. But not since I've been reading Rossetti. Oh, Mum—he's the most lovely poet. I've been reading him since six this morning.

DOROTHY. Now, Ann—you know I don't like you working before breakfast.

ANN. But the early morning's the best time for poetry—when

everything's fresh. The words get right inside you and your mind's so clear it's like—like crystal water.

DOROTHY. No wonder your brain feels as if it's floating.

ANN. Oh, Mum—don't be piggy. It's lovely to read aloud.

DOROTHY. Doesn't Cath object to your reading aloud?

ANN (*getting up off the bed and crossing to the door* R.). She was out this morning, soon after six—that's why she came back and bagged my bath.

DOROTHY. Do you mean she actually went out at six for a walk? The spring does seem to have broken out.

(ROGER *is heard singing in the bathroom.*)

ANN. Hark to Father—(*hurrying across and up* L.) he seems to have broken out too! (*At the bathroom door, but not opening it.*) I say, Daddy—would you like to hurry and lend me your bathroom? Would you?

(DOROTHY *says,* " Now, Ann," *at the same moment that an indistinct murmur is heard from* ROGER.)

But, darling, wouldn't you like to shave in your dressing-room?

ROGER (*in the bathroom*). NO.

ANN. Oh, do be a sport, Daddy. Cath's bagged the bathroom and I'm terribly late and——

ROGER (*grumblingly*). Oh, all right. I suppose I'm allowed to dry myself.

ANN. Oh, darling—you *are* a pet rabbit. (*To* DOROTHY.) He's going to let me. Whoops of joy.

DOROTHY. And what about my bath?

ANN. I'll only be a few minutes. Honest.—Oh, you don't really mind, do you? (*She flings herself at her mother.*) Darling Mummy face.

DOROTHY. I will not be called Mummy face. Of all the revolting——

ANN (*kneeling up on the bed*). But it's a term of endearment. Anyhow, Egyptian mummies are lovely—all queer and mysterious. (*With sudden complete self-absorption.*) Mummy, do you think I'm psychic?

DOROTHY (*discouragingly*). Why?

ANN. Well, I'm always feeling as if I ought to be able to see things. I expect it's because I'm sensitive. (*She picks up* DOROTHY'S *hand-mirror.*) I've got a sensitive mouth, haven't I, Mummy?

DOROTHY. I expect it's sensitive about the tooth inside it.

ANN. Oh, Mummy, I do think you're unromantic, just when I was talking about important things. You're always shrivelling me up. Do you know what I read in the paper yesterday? Girls of my age are like sensitive plants.

DOROTHY. Darling child, I didn't mean to shrivel you——

But there really are times when I'm afraid you're getting a bit morbid.

ANN. I wonder. I suppose a lot of great people have been morbid. Rossetti buried his poems in his wife's coffin. But then he dug them up. Mummy, if I die, I'd rather you didn't cremate me.

DOROTHY. Ann—you're not to talk like that. It's not a bit clever to be morbid.

(ANN *looks pained.*)

Oh, for goodness' sake don't get shrivelled again. You're not feeling ill, are you, darling?

ANN (*wistful, but resigned*). No, Mummy. Just a bit strange sometimes. I expect I've outgrown my strength.

DOROTHY. Then you couldn't have had much strength. You're only as big as tuppence-ha'-penny now. Silly baby. (*She catches* ANN's *hand and gives it an affectionate squeeze; then looks at it critically.*) Are you remembering to manicure your nails properly?

ANN (*snatching her hand away and rising*). No, Mum, you're not to look. To-day's their worst day.

DOROTHY (*firmly taking her hand*). Come on, now. Oh, Ann! Those cuticles haven't been done for weeks. Give me an orange stick. (*She makes a gesture towards the dressing-table.*)

ANN. No, Mummy, there isn't time—I'll be terribly late. (*She runs to the bathroom door.*) Daddy. Ow-ow! (*She howls like a dog.*) Oh dear—I wonder how far Cath's got. (*She runs to the door* R. *and opens it.*)

(ROGER *comes out of the bathroom, in a large bathrobe, carrying his shaving-tackle.*)

ROGER. Here you are, nuisance.

ANN (*running across* L., *having left the door ajar*). Oh, thank you, darling. You are a pet lamb. Roger! You've got a new bath-wrap!

DOROTHY. You are not to call your father Roger.

ANN. But he likes it, don't you, darling? And it's fashionable for children to treat their parents as if they were human.

ROGER (*crossing to between the beds*). Get along with you, baggage.

(ANN, *about to enter, turns back.*)

ANN. Mummy, can I have the weeniest squeedge of your bath salts?

DOROTHY. Well, use the ones in the big tin—not the Floris. I know your squeedges.

ANN. I'll only take one grain.

(*She goes in and shuts the door.*)

DOROTHY. Roger, do you think that child's all right?

ROGER. I should say she was bursting with health.

DOROTHY. She's getting the most extraordinary ideas—about death and poets.

ROGER. It's just a phase. You had it when we were engaged. (*He takes his watch from the bedside table.*) Good. I'll get five minutes in the garden if I sprint.

(DOROTHY *has resumed her spectacles and picked up* "The Times.")

What are you doing with "The Times."

DOROTHY. Reading it. Vera brought it up instead of the "Express."

ROGER. Well, for goodness' sake don't muck it about. I hate reading a paper after a woman's been at it.

(*He goes into his dressing-room, up* R., *leaving the door open, and starts to hum.*)

DOROTHY. Gertie Mills has had a baby.

ROGER (*invisible, shaving*). What?

DOROTHY. Gertie Mills has had a boy.

ROGER. Didn't know she was married. (*He comes to the doorway, lathering his face.*)

DOROTHY. Well, I should hardly think she'd announce the baby in "The Times" if she wasn't. Of course she's married. We sent her a fish-slice.

ROGER. Damned original of us.

DOROTHY. She asked for it.

ROGER. She's the sort of woman who would slice her fish.

(*He disappears again.*)

DOROTHY (*after turning page after page and scanning the headlines*). There seems to be nothing whatever in this paper.

ROGER (*coming to the doorway*). They just bring it out so that you can line drawers with it.

DOROTHY. I wish you'd close your door. There's a ghastly draught.

(ROGER *shuts the door.* DOROTHY *decides to fold the paper at the Woman's Page. Catastrophe overtakes "The Times," which flutters in several directions. She is about to collect the pages when she hears steps in the passage—the bedroom door is slightly open.*)

Catherine—is that you?

(MARTIN HILTON *enters* R., *a pleasant-looking boy of seventeen. He is in his dressing-gown.*)

MARTIN. No, it's me, darling. (*He crosses to* R. *of* DOROTHY's *bed.*)

DOROTHY. Oh, good morning, dear. (*She takes off her spectacles.*)

MARTIN (*kissing her*). Very fetching we're looking this morning with our head in a little string bag. Any chance of using your bathroom?

DOROTHY. Ann's in it. But Cath can't be long now.

MARTIN. Can't she just.

DOROTHY. You don't think she's fainted, do you?

MARTIN. Shouldn't be surprised. She might do anything these days. Never knew a girl so soppy. (*He sits* L. *on* DOROTHY'S *bed and picks up a page of* "*The Times.*") Anyhow, I don't care. I'm not really in a hurry.

DOROTHY. But you'll be late for breakfast and it's Vera's first morning. Really, one would think five people could share two baths without all this trouble. Go and bang on the door. Something really may have happened to her.

MARTIN. Oh, no, it hasn't. (*Dropping the paper.*) She told me to go to hell last time I banged. (*He suddenly flings himself across his mother's feet.*)

DOROTHY. Martin—for goodness' sake! Get off, you great lump. You don't know how heavy you are.

(MARTIN *shifts slightly down the bed.*)

No—really—you'll bust the hot-water bottle.

MARTIN. Hot-water bottle! (*He rises.*) What pampered creatures you women are. Hot-water bottle on a day like this!

DOROTHY. It wasn't a day like this last night. It was jolly cold.

MARTIN (*lying on* ROGER'S *bed*). And now spring has burst on an astonished world. (*He gives a violent squirm on the bed and then sits up.*) Talking of dogs, darling—is Father reconciled to my going away with Alistair at Easter?

DOROTHY. I'm afraid not, dear. I've done my best. But he doesn't really like Alistair—and when we've just got the new car—

MARTIN. And what a car. The dowagers' home of rest.

DOROTHY. Well, I like a car to be comfortable.

MARTIN. Darling, you're getting dreadfully plushy. At any moment you'll take to an ear-trumpet and eucalyptus pastilles. (*He performs more gymnastics on the bed, then springs up and crosses to the window.*) I think I ought to warn you, darling, that I shall go with Alistair whatever Father says.

DOROTHY. You must settle that yourself.

MARTIN (*looking through the window* ROGER *left open*). Dear, dear, something very nifty has broken out in the next-door garden.

DOROTHY. Yes, she's pretty.

MARTIN. Well, well. Frisking about like a young antelope. Girls are rather tripe, really.—Well, I'm damned! There's Cath sitting at the bathroom window.

DOROTHY. What's she doing?

MARTIN. Nothing whatever. Just looking completely blah.

(*Calling.*) Hi, there! Come out of it, you batty-looking hag——
(*He breaks off and draws back.*) Oh, my Lord—the vision next door thinks I mean her.
DOROTHY. Martin—really.
MARTIN. My dear—she's glaring like old boots—not at all a bad-looking gawk, really. What a lark!
DOROTHY. There's Cath coming out. (*Calling.*) Cath—come here a minute.
MARTIN (*turning and facing the door* R.). I'm just going to give her a piece of my mind.
(CATHERINE HILTON *enters* R., *wearing a dressing-gown over her under-clothes. She is just under nineteen, a really beautiful girl of unusual type, dark and intense and, at present, rather sullen.*)
CATHERINE. Yes, Mother?
MARTIN (*crossing* R.C. *to the foot of* ROGER'S *bed*). Of all the selfish, greedy——
CATHERINE (*passing below* MARTIN *to* C.). I'm not talking to you. (*She sits on the foot of* ROGER'S *bed.*)
MARTIN. But I'm talking to you. What do you think the rest of us are doing while you get stuck in a trance at the bath-room window? I suppose you think you looked like that Rossetti picture Ann's got over her bed.
CATHERINE. I don't look at Ann's pictures; and I wish she'd clear the rotten things out. I'm sick of sharing a bedroom. There's no privacy anywhere in this house.
MARTIN. So you thought you'd have a little privacy in the bathroom while two of us waited?
CATHERINE (*rising and crossing to the dressing-table*). Oh, shut up! It's bad enough having you about the house without listening to you. (*Sitting on the dressing-table stool.*) One minute you're just a grubby little schoolboy and the next minute you're trying to be Noel Coward, and both ways you're equally disgusting.
MARTIN. *Good* morning. There, you see, Mother—loopy. (*Crossing to* R. *of* CATHERINE.) You know what'll happen to you, my girl. They'll come for you in a van.
DOROTHY. Go and have your bath, dear.
MARTIN. Right you are. (*Still close to* CATHERINE.) Dear, dear —all that time in the bath and her neck's still dirty.

(CATHERINE *turns furiously.*)

(*Crossing* R.) Call Father if she gets dangerous.

(*He dashes out of the door* R., *banging it behind him.*)

CATHERINE (*rising*). Really, Mother—he's quite unbearable. (*Crossing up to* L. *of* DOROTHY'S *bed.*) You ought to speak to him.
DOROTHY. Well, dear, I was just going to speak to you. You really must be a little more considerate.

Sc. 1.] CALL IT A DAY. 29

CATHERINE. Heavens, just because I spent a few extra minutes in the bath.
DOROTHY. You took Ann's turn.
CATHERINE. My God, anyone would think we were at boarding-school.
DOROTHY. Cath, I will not have you saying "My God."
CATHERINE. But I've told you, Mother—it doesn't mean anything.
DOROTHY. Then there's no point in saying it. Oh, I know you don't mean to be blasphemous, dear, but——
CATHERINE. Look here—I'll make a bargain: if I stop saying "My God," will you let me have the spare bedroom?
DOROTHY. Now, Cath, we've gone into all this——
CATHERINE. I tell you I'll turn out if we have a visitor.
DOROTHY. But you'll always make a grievance of turning out—and leave things behind. Visitors simply hate finding grubby bits of powder-puffs in the drawers. No—I simply must keep the spare bedroom.
CATHERINE. Then I shall go on saying "My God."
DOROTHY. You've no right to make a religious question of it.
CATHERINE. I want the spare bedroom.
DOROTHY. What's wrong with your room? Is it Ann's early morning reading that upsets you?
CATHERINE. That and her early evening praying. She now says her prayers under a picture of Shelley.
DOROTHY. Do you mean she actually prays to it?
CATHERINE. Not exactly. She says that's the holiest part of the room.
DOROTHY. Shelley would be pleased.
CATHERINE. It isn't only Ann—it's just that I want to be alone.
DOROTHY. But why? I could understand if you were working—studying something.
CATHERINE. Well, perhaps I will take something up—if you give me the spare bedroom.
DOROTHY. No, Cath. I'm sorry, dear, but——
CATHERINE. You're not a bit sorry. You're the most un-understanding mother I've ever met. How can anyone be so beastly on a lovely day when everything—everything—— Oh God, how I hate this whole rotten house! (*She rushes out* R., *slamming the door after her.*)
DOROTHY (*torn between wrath and concern*). Catherine, come back this instant. (*She springs out of bed, picks up her dressing-gown and goes to the door* R.) Cath—Cath dear——

(CATHERINE'S *door slams.* ROGER *comes from the dressing-room.*)

ROGER. Did you call, Dot?
DOROTHY. No, dear—not you. (*Looking after* CATHERINE.) Really, there must be something wrong with her. (*She puts on her dressing-gown.*)

ROGER. Oh, rot! I tell you it's just a phase. (*He crosses to the table between the beds and puts things in his pockets.*)
DOROTHY. It's not Ann now—it's Cath. I never heard such an outburst. Just because I won't give her the spare bedroom.

(ANN *enters from the bathroom.*)

Ann, have you noticed anything wrong with Cath? (*She crosses to the foot of her bed and puts on mules.*)
ANN (*after a second's pause*). No, darling. I think she's quite all right. (*She crosses to the door* R.)
DOROTHY. Is she sleeping well?
ANN. I—I think so. Skuse me, darling. I'm frabjously late.

(*She scuttles out.*)

DOROTHY. Roger, that child was hiding something.
ROGER. Rubbish. You fuss over them too much.
DOROTHY. But if you'd heard Cath. (*She sits on the* R. *side of her bed.*)
ROGER. She's always had a bit of a temper. Why not let her have the spare room?
DOROTHY. And what about your mother and your sisters?
ROGER. Let 'em go to an hotel. (*He crosses to the dressing-table and starts hunting in the drawer.*)
DOROTHY. I'd like to see your face if I suggested it. What are you doing in that drawer?
ROGER. Thought perhaps some of my linen handkerchiefs had got in by mistake.
DOROTHY. Of course they haven't. (*As he takes one.*) Now, Roger—that's one of the large ones I keep for my colds.
ROGER. Well, you haven't got a cold now, have you, old lady? (*He grins and pockets the handkerchief, then crosses to her and kisses her.*)
DOROTHY. What on earth you do with your handkerchiefs——. No, it's no use. I'm sure I oughtn't to give in to her. It's not natural—this longing to be alone.
ROGER. Oh, yes it is—(*crossing to the window*) everyone feels it sometimes. (*He gazes out of the window for a second; then jerks back.*) Well, I'm going to have five minutes' run.
DOROTHY. Now for goodness' sake don't keep breakfast waiting on Vera's first morning.
ROGER. All right—all right. I'm only going in the garden. (*He pulls his coat down in front of the mirror on the dressing-table.*)
DOROTHY. Did you try those scales?

(ROGER *hums, crossing to the door* R.)

I said, did you try those scales?
ROGER. What?—Oh, yes. The rotten things never were correct. (*He catches sight of the dishevelled "Times."*) My God, look at that paper!

DOROTHY. Oh, don't fuss. I'll put it straight.
ROGER. Like hell you will. No woman ought to be trusted alone with " The Times."
DOROTHY (*battling with the fallen sheets*). I think very few women would want to be. Oh, run along and don't be late.
ROGER. You're in a very bossy mood. Look at the weather, woman, and relax—relax.
(*He goes out* R. DOROTHY *continues to wrestle with* " *The Times,*" *getting it into some sort of order.* MARTIN *puts his head round the door* R.)
MARTIN. It may interest you to know that my bath was stone cold.
DOROTHY. If anyone else mentions the word bath I shall go raving mad.
MARTIN. Sorry, lady, but facts is facts. (*He disappears, closing the door.*)
(DOROTHY *crosses hurriedly to the bathroom door.*)

CURTAIN.

SCENE 2

SCENE.—*The Kitchen.* 8.30 *a.m.*
Once Victorian, it has been greatly modernized, with white painted walls, blue and white lino, check curtains and tablecloth. A highly coloured nursery picture of cows hangs over the mantelpiece. A window and a door leading to the garden are on the left wall, a sink in front of the window. A dresser and an electric stove are on the right wall, and an old-fashioned range is centre of the back wall with a kitchen cabinet on its R. *and a door on its* L. *A large table and chairs are* C., *the table laid for three and with a tray of egg-cups, etc., on it ready to go upstairs. A large number of small properties, such as kitchen canisters, crockery, etc., as required.*
(*See Photograph of Scene.*)

When the CURTAIN *rises,* VERA *is minding the toast on the stove.* COOK, *a buxom, middle-aged woman, is warming a teapot from the kettle on the range.*

COOK. How many pieces have you done?
VERA (*counting the toast in the racks on the electric cooker*). Eight.
COOK. Two more'll do it. Time those eggs came off. (*She lifts the saucepan from the range to one side.*)
VERA. That clock's said twenty-five past for ever so long.
COOK (*taking the clock from the mantelpiece*). Drat it, it's stopped —and no wonder. You've been and stood it the right way up.

That clock only goes on its side. (*She puts the clock on its side.*) You'd better run up and look at the hall clock.

(VERA *gives a glance at the toast on the griller and goes off up* L. COOK *crosses to the sink and empties the teapot.* ROGER *comes in down* L. *from the garden.*)

ROGER (*calling into the garden*). Hi, Terry—come along there. Breakfast.

COOK. Not on my clean floor, please, sir. He's been on the flower-beds.

ROGER. Oh, all right. I'll give it to him in the garden. (*He goes to the sink, on the drainer of which the dog's breakfast is standing.*) Weet-meet? That's right. And a little milk. (*He gets it from the tray on the table* C.)

COOK (*at the range again*). Wait and I'll give you a drop of bacon fat, sir.

ROGER (*pouring milk*). Certainly not. He's too fat already. Where are his hard biscuits? (*He puts the milk-jug on the drainer.*)

COOK. We're out of them, sir, and he doesn't like them.

ROGER. I daresay not, but they're good for his teeth. No woman can be trusted to feed a dog properly. You get some of those biscuits in.

COOK (*filling the teapot at the range*). Very good, sir, but he won't eat them.

ROGER. He'll eat them if he's not pampered.

(VERA *returns from up* L.)

You're not to give Terry scraps in the kitchen; do you understand, Vera?

VERA. No, sir, of course not.

ROGER. Poor little chap's getting a stomach like a barrel. (*Going through the door to the garden.*) Hi, there! Good man!

COOK (*calling after him*). Breakfast's just going up, sir. Potty about that dog he is.

VERA (*down* L.). Nice, I call that.

COOK (*filling the hot-water jug at the range*). Oh, he's all right, but you got to be firm with him. She's just the opposite, you have to humour her.

VERA. I must say, she's very familiar like.

COOK. That's her way. (*Putting the hot-water jug on the tray.*) She's not bad if you know how to manage her. What time was it?

VERA. Twenty-five to.

COOK. Lord, we're late. (*She puts the teapot on the tray.*) Where's that toast? (*She takes the eggs from the range.*)

VERA (*with a squeal*). Ow, I forgot it. (*She rushes* R. *to the stove and takes out two burnt pieces.*)

COOK. It'll do—with a scrape. And put it in the middle of the rack. (*Taking eggs from the saucepan and putting them into the*

egg-cups on the tray.) They don't always finish it. Which of these eggs is the master's?
VERA (*scraping toast*). Lor'—if I didn't forget to mark them.
COOK (*replacing the saucepan on the range*). You're a nice one. Told you plain as plain—five minutes for the master's or there'll be ructions. Oh, well, I'll put a cross on the two brown ones. (*She marks them with a pencil.*) If he says anything you can say they was very new laid.
VERA. I am sorry, Cook. (*She puts the toast racks on the tray.*)
COOK. Where's the sugar?

(VERA *runs to the kitchen cabinet* R.C. *and takes canister marked* "*Sugar*.")

No—not there. Sugar's in "Sago."
VERA (*going back to the cabinet and replacing* "*Sugar*"). Oh, I see. (*She takes down* "*Sago*.") What's sago in?
COOK. Sago's in that little old tin of Cadbury's cocoa.

(VERA *pours sugar into the bowl on the tray.*)

(*As* VERA *picks up the tray.*) Now have you got everything? Tea, hot water, sugar, toast, eggs—where's that milk? (*She gets it from the drainer by the window and puts it on the tray.*) Be careful, now.

(COOK *opens the door up* L. *and* VERA *takes the tray out.*)

(*Calling after her.*) Mind that top step. It's awkward like. (*She turns to the range and makes the kitchen tea.*)

(MRS. MILSOM, *a small bird-like charwoman, comes in from the garden entrance. Her invariably gloomy sentiments are delivered with a surprising briskness.*)

MRS. MILSOM (L.). Morning, Mrs. Hawkins. Treacherous sort of day.
COOK (*filling the kitchen tea-pot*). Looks all right to me.
MRS. MILSOM (*taking the apron from the peg on the door down* L. *and hanging her coat up in its place*). Yes. It looks all right. That's what's wrong with it. It tempts people. They go leaving things off. There'll be some pewmonia about next week. (*She puts on the apron.*)
COOK (*at the range*). How's your husband?
MRS. MILSOM (*crossing* R.). Bad. He looks better and he says he feels better. But I *know*. Gone back to work, he has.
COOK (*going to the oven*). Well, that's a good job.
MRS. MILSOM. So you might think. But like as not he'll have to come home in a cab—if not something worse.
COOK (*opening the oven door and taking out a dish of bacon*). How do you mean, worse? (*She brings the bacon to the table.*)

Mrs. Milsom (R. *of the table*). I said to him before he went, "One of these days you'll come home feet first." Is that a bit of bacon?

Cook (*sitting in the chair above the table*). Yes. Want to make yourself some toast?

Mrs. Milsom. No, bread'll do. (*She sits in the chair* R. *of the table.*) I like a bit of bacon. Though I sometimes wonder at you eating it.

Cook. Why?

Mrs. Milsom (*buttering bread*). Blood pressure.

Cook. What do you mean, blood pressure?

Mrs. Milsom. You got it, haven't you?

Cook (*pouring out tea*). First I've heard of it.

Mrs. Milsom. You're just the right build for it. My sister-in-law's had it something shocking. Doctor told her if she touched a bit of bacon she might drop down dead.

Cook. Bacon's never done me any harm. (*She is about to help herself; then stops.*) What's the blood press on?

Mrs. Milsom (*cutting bread*). Everything. All the time. Do you get noises in your head?

Cook. No.

Mrs. Milsom. Well, you can have blood pressure without that. (*She helps herself to bacon.*) Do your legs swell?

Cook. A bit. But they always did.

Mrs. Milsom. P'raps you always had it. Lots of people never know anything about it till they has a stroke.

Cook. Well, you are a nice cup of tea. How do they cure it?

Mrs. Milsom (*eating*). Knocks you off things.

Cook. What things?

Mrs. Milsom. Most things. Gets you down to skin and bone. They got my sister-in-law down to six stone two. Completely cured, she was. She's got anæmia now. You eating that bit of bacon?

Cook. I don't know that I am. But there's Vera yet. Oh, well, she can do herself some more.

(Mrs. Milsom *helps herself.*)

My legs have been bad this last month. Do you think I ought to see a doctor?

Mrs. Milsom (*pouring tea*). Doctors can't always tell. But you might as well. If he doesn't find that he may find something else.

(Vera *returns, up* L.)

Cook. Oh, Vera, this is Mrs. Milsom.

Vera (L. *of the table*). Pleased to meet you. I say, Cook, the master went and picked the very worst bit of toast. I did feel awful. (*She crosses and puts the tray on the floor* R., *leaning it against the downstage end of the dresser.*)

Sc. 2.] CALL IT A DAY. 35

Cook (*pouring out* Vera's *tea*). You'd have felt worse if the missus had picked it. They started those eggs yet?
Vera. Just as I came out.
Cook. Oh, well. Want to do yourself a bit of bacon?
Vera. No, thanks. Got any corn-flakes?
Cook. We did have some. Now, let me see—yes, on the shelf with the dog biscuits.

(Vera *discovers corn-flakes in lower cupboard of kitchen cabinet,* R.C*, also bringing to light a bottle of ink.*)

Well, if that isn't my bottle of ink. Put it on the dresser, will you? I like to have things in their right place. (*She is pouring herself out more tea.*) I suppose tea isn't bad for blood pressure?

(Vera *puts the ink on the dresser and returns to* L. *of the table with a plate of flakes.*)

Mrs. Milsom. Worst thing out.
Cook (*drinking*). Well, it'll take more than blood pressure to put me off tea.

(Vera, *seated* L. *of the table, has settled to her breakfast All three stir their tea. Suddenly a bell rings and the indicator over the door works.*)

If that's the eggs, there won't be any more till the boy comes.
Vera. Oh lor'.

(*She rises and goes off up* L. Cook *rises, bangs the indicator with a hearth brush, and returns to her chair.*)

Mrs. Milsom. What's she like?
Cook. Oh, not bad.
Mrs. Milsom. She'll make more work for you. Young ones always do. Will she help me turn the dining-room out, same as Susan?
Cook (*cutting bread*). Well, it's not really her work.

(Vera *returns.*)

Was it the eggs?
Vera. No. Slop-basin.

(*She gets it from the dresser and goes out again.*)

Mrs. Milsom (*reading the paper*). Fancy ringing for that. (*She holds out her cup.*) Hot it up a bit, will you.—Did Mrs. Hilton say it wasn't her work?
Cook (*pouring tea into* Mrs. Milsom's *cup*). It never was Susan's work.
Mrs. Milsom. Well, I can't do a room by myself in a morning. I'm not a steam-engine.
Cook. You'd better see if you can get round her.

(Vera *returns.*)

Mrs. Milsom. Come and sit down.

(Vera *sits* l. *of the table again.*)

They got no consideration, running you off your feet like that. Have a drop more milk?

Vera (*pouring milk on to her corn-flakes*). Thanks ever so.

Mrs. Milsom. Nice to see a bright young face about the house.

Vera. There are some bright young faces upstairs and no mistake. My word, that Catherine hasn't half got a nasty temper.

Cook. What's wrong with her?

Vera. Well, the master was going on about his egg being soft, and suddenly she says, " Oh, for God's sake "—she did really— " for God's sake, take mine. What does the beastly egg matter— what does anything matter?" And out she goes, slamming the door.

Mrs. Milsom. Well?

Cook. And did the master take the egg?

Vera. Yes.

Cook. Well, that's saved us a bit of trouble.

Vera. Fancy speaking like that!

(Mrs. Milsom, *having finished her bacon, takes marmalade.*)

Cook. If you ask me, Miss Cath's head's been getting a bit turned, having her portrait painted and what not.

Vera. Anyone can have their portrait painted.

Cook. If they pay for it. But they're doing her for nothing. This man wrote to the master and said he'd like to have the privilege of painting his daughter because she was the most beautiful English girl he'd seen for years. Susan happened to catch sight of the letter.

Vera. Well, she's not my idea of beauty.

Cook. He's a famous artist. The missus says it'll probably be bought for the nation.

Mrs. Milsom. I'm surprised at Mrs. Hilton letting Miss Cath sit for an artist. I cleaned for a couple of them once. (*She takes more marmalade.*)

Vera. Was it awful?

Mrs. Milsom. Well, it was and it wasn't. I'll say this for them. They wasn't fussy about the cleaning.

Cook. I like Miss Cath, even if she has got a bit of a paddy.

Mrs. Milsom. She always was your favourite.

Vera. The master's mine. (*She helps herself to marmalade.*)

Cook (*passing the bread to* Vera). You've made up your mind quickly.

Vera. What does he do?

Cook. He's an accountant.

Vera. Is that all?

Cook. He's charted, of course.

VERA. Oh! (*She cuts herself a slice of bread.*)
MRS. MILSOM. What *is* a charted accountant.
COOK. A man who charts accounts, of course. It's sort of book-keeping.
VERA. What's Martin do?
COOK. He's studying for exams. He's going into his father's office after Easter.
VERA. Not much to look at, is he? I like dark men myself. Cook, who does that bulldog belong to?
COOK (*drinking tea*). What bulldog?
VERA. I saw one at the end of the road—when I took Terry out.
MRS. MILSOM. You keep away from it. If it once gets hold of Terry, it'll never let go. They can't.
VERA. What, never?
MRS. MILSOM. Course not. It's the way their jaws are made.
COOK. Oh, don't talk so silly. It couldn't spend the rest of its life with a dog in its mouth, could it?—It belongs to that big corner house. Why?
VERA. I just wondered.
COOK. Was there a tall dark man with it?
VERA. Yes—I believe there was.
COOK. That's their butler. Nice-looking chap.
VERA. Is he? I didn't notice.

(*Both look at her.*)

(*Suddenly getting flustered.*) I say, that's a funny sort of picture.
COOK (*looking at the picture of the cows*). You may well say so. Came out of the nursery. "Cook," she says, "this'll brighten the kitchen up." Fancy giving me a picture of cows. As if I didn't see enough of beef.
VERA. Funny sort of curtains, aren't they?
COOK. Bed ticking, if you ask me. We used to have some decent red ones. Do you remember those plush curtains, Mrs. Milsom?
MRS. MILSOM. Yes. They was curtains, they was.
COOK (*drinking*). I like a kitchen to look like a kitchen. Still, you got to humour her. (*Rising.*) We'd better get a move on. Want this bit of bacon fat?
MRS. MILSOM. No, thanks.
COOK. The dog can have it, then.
VERA (*rising*). But the master said——
COOK. Oh, he says a lot. There's a bit of marmalade, too. Terry likes marmalade. You can give it him on the step. (*She scrapes the scraps on to* VERA'S *plate.*)
VERA. Well, I suppose it's all right.

(*She takes the plate and goes into the garden down* L.)

MRS. MILSOM. She's got her eyes open.
COOK. Bulldogs, indeed. 'Course he's a good-looking chap.
MRS. MILSOM. Look at her, frisking about on the grass with Terry. Shouldn't wonder if you didn't have trouble with her.
COOK (*crossing with plates to the sink*). I'll watch her.

(*The bell rings.* VERA *comes in.*)

They're ringing for you to clear.
VERA (*crossing* R.). My word, they have been quick. (*She smooths her hair and picks up the tray.*) It's ever such a lovely day.
MRS. MILSOM. You going to give me a bit of a hand with that dining-room? You could do the paint round the window. Then you could look out.
COOK. That bulldog might come along.

(*She laughs uproariously,* MRS. MILSOM *joining her with a hen-like cackle.*)

VERA. I don't want to see no bulldogs.

(*The bell rings again.*)

(*Crossing* L.) Gracious, what's wrong with them?

(*She goes off up* L.)

(*The bell rings again, furiously.* COOK *drops a plate in the sink and breaks it, then philosophically puts the broken pieces into the dustbin under the sink. She then slithers the crockery noisily into the sink, singing meanwhile "I'm for ever blowing bubbles."*)

CURTAIN.

SCENE 3

SCENE.—*The Dining-room.* 8.55 a.m.
A pleasant, rather conventional room. The door is upstage in the L. *wall. The window is in the* R. *wall, with a sideboard above it. The fireplace is in the* L. *wall, below the door. The table is* C.
(*See Photograph of Scene.*)

When the CURTAIN *rises,* ROGER *is seated* R. *of the table reading some letters;* DOROTHY, *seated* L. *of the table, has a draper's catalogue;* MARTIN, *in the chair* L. *of* ROGER, *has a large pile of motor catalogues.* ANN *is below the fireplace, ringing the bell furiously.*

DOROTHY. Ann, stop at once. Ringing the bell like that! Whatever will Vera think?
ANN (*crossing* R.). Oh, why doesn't she come! Why doesn't someone do something? Oh, it must be somewhere! (*Rushing at* ROGER.) Daddy, are you sure you're not sitting on it?

Sc. 3.]   CALL IT A DAY.   39

ROGER. I'm not sitting on anything I oughtn't to be sitting on. (*He passes his cup to* DOROTHY.)

(VERA *enters with the tray.*)

DOROTHY. I'm sorry, Vera, we're not ready for you to clear yet. It's Miss Ann's exercise book. You haven't seen it, have you? (*She pours out tea into* ROGER'S *cup.*)

ANN. My algebra exercise book—it's got a green cover. I had it a minute ago. Do you think you took it down with you?

VERA. I haven't set eyes on it, miss.

DOROTHY. Of course she hasn't. Do control yourself, Ann. Thank you, Vera.

(VERA *goes.*)

ANN (*crossing* L. *in front of table*). Oh Heavens! (*She is turning the room upside down.*)

DOROTHY. You'll have to go without it. (*She gives* ROGER *his cup.*)

ANN (*going to the books* L.). I can't go without it. No one's ever lost an exercise book. (*At the armchair* L.). Oh, can't someone do something?

DOROTHY. Now stop getting excited. (*She rises.*) Where were you sitting?

ANN. Here on the floor.

DOROTHY. And then at the table. Martin, are you sure it isn't in your catalogue?

MARTIN. I've looked, I tell you.

ANN (*nearly in tears*). Oh, Mummy!

DOROTHY. We'll look again. (*She shakes the catalogue.*) Nothing there, nothing there—is this it? (*It is shut up in a big catalogue. She gives it to* ANN.)

ANN. Martin, you utterly beastly beast. I asked you. (*She crosses to* MARTIN *and beats him on the head with the exercise book.*)

MARTIN. Here, cut it out.

(ROGER *tears up letters.*)

ANN (*crossing* L.). You and your rotten motor catalogues, when you haven't enough money to buy a scooter. (*She opens the exercise book on the floor in front of the chair down* L.)

DOROTHY. Come and finish your breakfast.

ANN. But I've just thought how to do it.

DOROTHY. Well, eat this then. (*She gives* ANN *a slice of toast with marmalade on it.*)

ANN (*taking it and glancing at the clock on the mantelpiece*). Golly, I've only got five minutes. Oh, Mum, the marmalade's dripped on it. Whatever will Miss Fry think?

DOROTHY. Here, give it to me.

(ANN *passes the exercise book over.* DOROTHY *dips her napkin in the hot-water jug and sponges the book.*)

You'd better go and get your hat on. You can finish this in the train.

(*A clock outside strikes nine.*)

ANN (*giving a horrible howl*). Mummy!

ROGER. What on earth——

ANN. It's striking! That clock's ten minutes slow.

DOROTHY (*giving the book back to* ANN). Oh, good heavens—Vera doesn't know about putting it on every morning. I must remember to tell her about the hall clock, too.

ANN. But you don't seem to understand. I shall be late.

DOROTHY. Well, you'll have to be late for once.

ANN. I can't be late. No one ever is . . . (*She is putting her books together.*)

MARTIN. Yours is the rummiest school. They never do anything to you and you all behave like lambs. What happens if you make a row during class?

ANN. I've told you. You get a report.

MARTIN. And what do you do with it?

ANN. You take it to your form mistress.

MARTIN. And what does she do with it?

ANN. She doesn't do anything with it. (*Doing up her books.*) Oh, don't keep asking silly questions. You just *can't* keep getting reports.

MARTIN. You must be a lot of blooming little angels.

DOROTHY. Oh, don't tease her, Martin.—How late will you be?

ANN. I tell you I can't be late. I'll have to take a taxi.

DOROTHY. You'll do no such thing.

ANN. I'll pay for it myself.

DOROTHY. I shall not allow you to spend your money on taxis to school. It's ridiculous.

ANN. But, Mummy——

DOROTHY. No, Ann. I forbid it. It would cost at least five shillings.

(MARTIN *passes his cup, which* DOROTHY *refills.*)

ANN (*crossing* R. *above the table*). Oh, Daddy, please—I can't be late. Please make her let me.

ROGER. Can't do that, old lady.—Tell you what, put on your bonnet and I'll run you down in the car.

ANN (*with a squeal*). Darling! (*Running* L. *again.*) Oh, you angel lamb. Then we needn't start for five minutes. Oh, what a father to have! Where's that algebra? (*She lies on the floor working.*)

DOROTHY. Roger! You never use the car in the mornings. (*She hands* MARTIN *his cup.*)

ROGER (*taking the paper from the chair below the table*). I feel like it to-day. Might drive back through the Park. You don't want it, do you?

DOROTHY. Oh no. I'm spending the day with Muriel Weston.
ROGER. Rather you than me. Lord, how that woman talks.
DOROTHY. We're going to shop this morning and do a matinée this afternoon. And then we're going to tea at her brother's rooms.
ROGER. Didn't know she had a brother.
DOROTHY. He's been rubber planting for years.
ROGER. What matinée are you going to ?
DOROTHY. A special show Fawcett's putting on. I want to see this new girl he's discovered.
ROGER. What, Beatrice Gwynne ? Are you sure there's a matinée to-day ?
DOROTHY. Why shouldn't there be ?
ROGER. She's coming to see us about her income tax. But her appointment's pretty late. I suppose the matinée will be over.
DOROTHY. Rather small fry for you, isn't she ?
ROGER. Fawcett asked us to look after her. She's got herself into some jam over her American earnings. (*He has been searching " The Times " as he talks.*) Oh, my Lord, Dorothy, this is a jig-saw puzzle, not a morning paper. Where's the financial page ?
DOROTHY. It just may have got under my bed. (*Half-rising.*) I'll get it.
ROGER (*putting the paper down*). No, thanks. (*He rises.*) Cut along, infant, and get your things on. (*He crosses above the table.*)
ANN. Right, darling one.

(*She gets up and goes out.*)

ROGER (*taking his pipe to the hearth and speaking to* MARTIN, *who is immersed in catalogues*). I should get a Rolls-Royce if I were you. Why you should burden the postman——
MARTIN (*loftily*). If you want to know, Alistair's mother has asked my advice about her new car. He's coming over to discuss it this afternoon. She may quite possibly get a Rolls.
ROGER (*filling his pipe*). Well, if you could bring yourself down to our lowly state of life, perhaps you'd go and start the Morris.
MARTIN (*with dignity*). Certainly.

(*He picks up the catalogues and goes out.*)

ROGER. I say, Dorothy, can't you do something about this Alistair business ?
DOROTHY (*eating*). But what can I do ? He's a charming boy.
ROGER. Like hell he is !
DOROTHY. I really do think you're most unjust about him. His mother's one of my oldest friends.
ROGER. Now, look here, you know exactly what I think of Alistair——
DOROTHY. Stuff and nonsense ! Just because the boy isn't rough and wild ! He's an excellent influence for Martin. If you

want to know, it's Cath I'm worried about. Roger, are you sure Paul Francis is all right?

ROGER. He's one of the best artists living, if that's what you mean.

DOROTHY. It certainly isn't. I mean—well, you know what his reputation is.

ROGER. Grossly exaggerated. You've met his wife—they're perfectly happy. You surely don't imagine——

DOROTHY. Well, Cath's behaving so queerly. If he were making love to her——

ROGER (*lighting his pipe*). My dear old girl, you're crazy. Even if he is a bit of a lad she'd be as safe as houses with him. I've known him thirty years. I was at school with him.

DOROTHY. Well, I was at school with Alistair's mother.

ROGER. That's neither here nor there.—You're just a fussy old lady. There's nothing wrong with the girl but a bit of temperament.

(ANN *enters.*)

ANN. Car's waiting, Daddy.

ROGER. Right.

ANN (*crossing to the window*). Do you know it's the most marvellous day. I feel as if something terribly exciting was going to happen. I'm psychic, you know.

(ROGER *gives a chuckle, then turns to* DOROTHY.)

ROGER (*kissing* DOROTHY). Good-bye, darling, don't fuss. (*Going up to the door.*) Enjoy your matinée. I wonder if that Gwynne girl will keep her appointment?

DOROTHY. Don't forget your paper.

ROGER. No, thanks. I'll get one that hasn't been woman-handled.

(*He goes out.* ANN *follows.*)

DOROTHY. Ann! Ann, come back and kiss me good-bye.

ANN (*returning*). Certainly, if you wish it. (*Coldly, she presents her cheek.*)

DOROTHY. Is this because I wouldn't let you take a taxi?

(ANN *does not answer, but sets her jaw.*)

Oh well, if you want to sulk.

ROGER (*calling*). Come on, Ann.

DOROTHY. Oh, get along with you.

(ANN *goes.* DOROTHY *gives a sigh, puts her letters together and tears an illustration from the draper's catalogue. Then she rises, goes to the fireplace and rings the bell.* CATHERINE *enters.* DOROTHY *takes a cigarette from the box on the mantelpiece and lights it.*)

CATHERINE (*below the table, feeling the teapot*). This stuff's cold. Can I have some fresh?

DOROTHY. Certainly not. Breakfast's over. The maids have their work to do.

CATHERINE. Oh, all right. (*She turns to go.*)

DOROTHY (*in a much kinder tone*). Cath, what *is* the matter with you?

CATHERINE. Nothing's the matter with me.

DOROTHY. But there must be something. You've been so restless and discontented lately. Why don't you take something up?

CATHERINE. What *can* I take up? I'm no good at anything. I suppose I could go on the stage.

DOROTHY. Have you got a sitting this afternoon?

CATHERINE. Yes.

DOROTHY. I suppose Mr. Francis isn't—there's nothing——

CATHERINE. What do you mean?

DOROTHY. Well, sometimes married men——

CATHERINE. Mother, how can you? I think you've got a thoroughly nasty mind. If you want to know, Mrs. Francis is there nearly all the time.

DOROTHY. Oh well, I'm sorry. But really——

(VERA *enters with a tray.* CATHERINE *dashes out.*)

(*Assuming a bright, cheerful manner.*) Yes, Vera, you can clear now. I think there must have been some muddle about the eggs this morning. The master's were both soft, and Miss Catherine's and mine were quite hard. I expect you got them mixed.

VERA. Yes, madam. I'm ever so sorry.

DOROTHY. You'll soon get used to our ways. I'll just go down and see Cook. I shall be out to lunch. (*She goes towards the door.*) Oh, if Mrs. Weston comes, ask her to go on up into my room, will you?

VERA. Yes, madam.

(DOROTHY *goes out.* VERA *pushes in* MARTIN'S *chair and is about to clear the table when she is attracted by the sunny window. She crosses to the chair* R., *kneels, and looks out.* MRS. MILSOM *enters with a Hoover.*)

MRS. MILSOM. You looking for that bulldog? (*She gives what she considers to be a satirical laugh.*)

VERA. Ooh, you didn't half startle me. I say, I didn't know they'd got a Hoover. That's nice.

MRS. MILSOM. Hm! You have to do a lot of walking with them.

VERA. I was looking at that tree. It's nearly out. Chestnut, isn't it?

MRS. MILSOM (*kneeling* R. *of the fireplace to plug in the Hoover*). Yes. They always come out first. More fools them.

VERA (*moving back to the table*). My word, it is a lovely day. Makes you feel quite different, doesn't it?

MRS. MILSOM. There'll be a lot of folk feel different before it's over.

VERA. Oh, get along with you. (*She begins clearing the breakfast things.*) A day like this does everyone good. Makes you feel you could do anything.

MRS. MILSOM. That's just it. Puts ideas into people's heads.

"The first Spring day
Is in the Devil's pay."

You never heard that?

(*A bell rings.*)

VERA. That'll be Mrs. Weston.

(*She hurries out.* MRS. MILSOM, *down* L., *turns the Hoover on. It whirs loudly. Slowly she pushes it across the stage as*

The CURTAIN *falls.*)

ACT II

Scene 1

Scene.—Paul Francis's *studio in Holland Park—originally the studio of* Paul's *father. 4.45 p.m.*

It still retains a rich Victorian atmosphere. Paintings in the pre-Raphaelite manner jostle modern canvases on the dark walls. There are books, flowers, draperies—a varied and colourful medley, where two utterly diverging schools of painting have met and grown accustomed to each other. There is a big north window at the back and a door L. *in the back wall.*

(*See Photograph of Scene.*)

When the Curtain *rises,* Paul, *a handsome, florid man of forty-five, is at his easel by the window. His wife* Ethel *is sitting on the settee* R. *She might be an old thirty or a young fifty. As a girl she must have had a small pleasant face; she is now the quintessence of the nondescript. But a close scrutiny would reveal that she is no fool. She is knitting something grey.*

Catherine Hilton *is seated on the model's throne,* L. *She wears a deep wine-coloured silk dress with tight bodice and full skirt. A very old olive-green shawl is draped across her shoulders. A book lies open on her knee.*

For a few moments Paul *paints.* Catherine *gazes at him. Every time he looks at her she drops her eyes to her book, only to look up at him again the minute he turns to his work.*

Paul. Don't keep looking up, Catherine. It takes you half a minute to get your face into repose again. Just forget all about me and read your book.

Ethel. Perhaps it isn't a very interesting book.

Catherine. It's all right. I just don't feel like reading.

Paul. Then just look down. (*As* Catherine *obeys.*) No, that's no good. You look as if you didn't even know *how* to read. My dear child, I want your face in repose, I don't want it wooden.

Ethel. Perhaps she wants a rest.

Paul. Nonsense. She had a rest five minutes ago. What's the matter? Have you got a pain?

(Catherine *turns her head, frowns and sets her jaw.* Ethel *is shaking her head at* Paul, *warning him to stop.*)

Oh hell, I'll have a shot at the shawl. Do what you like with your face, young woman.

CATHERINE. Would it be possible for you to paint the shawl without me in it?
PAUL. It would not.
ETHEL. If she wants to rest, Paul——
CATHERINE. I don't want to rest. But the beastly thing smells disgusting. I don't think you've any right to expect me to wear things you pick up in back streets.
ETHEL. It *is* rather dirty, Paul.
PAUL. Nonsense. It's perfect. It's pulled the whole thing together.
ETHEL (*suddenly*). Was that the bell?
PAUL. No. Don't fidget.
ETHEL. But it's Cook's day out. And Mary's just slipped out to change my book—— (*She rises.*)
PAUL. Never mind. You just stay where you are. Bobbing up and bobbing down!

(ETHEL *sits again.*)

Here, come here a minute.

(ETHEL *rises and goes to him.*)

Do you see what I mean—when she's got her lip stuck out like that? She's got a look of Tilly what's-it—the girl at St. Ives.
ETHEL. Tilly Marchmont?—No, I don't get it. (*She returns to the settee.*)
PAUL. Funny. It's gone now. Marchmont—that was it. Wonder if she's dead?
ETHEL. Why should she be dead?
PAUL. I dunno. She was a violent sort of girl. Yes, I bet she's dead all right. God, wasn't she beautiful that first year—before she went and got herself sunburnt? Shall I ever forget it! Coming into the studio with her arms and legs dark brown and her body pale pink. The most indecent sight. (*He laughs noisily.*) Do you remember?
ETHEL. I wasn't in that afternoon.
PAUL (*remembering*). No. So you weren't. Lord, I was mad with her—at first. (*He pauses for a second.*) After that she tried to get herself brown all over and nearly got run in by the police.
ETHEL (*laughing*). Poor Tilly.
PAUL. She wasn't poor. She was damn well off. She gave me a gold cigarette-case. Ethel, what happened to that cigarette-case?
ETHEL. I don't know, dear. I'll look for it.
PAUL. Tilly Marchmont. (*He gazes at* CATHERINE.) I'm getting it again now. Only the head, though. Cath's figure isn't a patch on hers.
ETHEL. I'm sure Cath's got a very nice figure.
PAUL. Don't be an ass, Ethel. You know perfectly well that

these girls with slim modern figures look like the wrath of God in the nude. (*Remembering again.*) Tilly had damn near the best body 1 ever saw. I'd like to paint her again.

ETHEL. Do you want me to find her?

PAUL. No. She'll be past her best now—look like one of Renoir's boiled ladies. I wonder what happened to her. She *was* a violent girl. I bet she's dead. (*Suddenly.*) Hey, I've got an idea. Catherine, put that shawl right over your head—cover all your hair up.

CATHERINE. I won't.

PAUL. What do you mean, you won't?

CATHERINE (*rising*). The thing's filthy. I won't put it on my head. I won't have it near me any longer. (*She throws the shawl down and kicks it away.*) There!

PAUL (*hurrying to her*). Yey—you'll damage it. It's dropping to pieces already. (*He picks it up, smooths it and goes towards* CATHERINE.) Now, look here, young woman——

CATHERINE (*backing* L.). Don't you come near me with that thing. Don't you dare——

(PAUL *is about to put the shawl round her.*)

ETHEL. Paul!

CATHERINE. You're not paying me for these sittings——

PAUL (L.). Paying you! I only pay people who know their job.

CATHERINE. I'm sorry I can't offer you gold cigarette-cases——

PAUL. Damn you, Catherine!

(ETHEL *rises.*)

CATHERINE (*suddenly snatching the shawl and tearing it fiercely*). There! (*She flings it away.*) I'm going home.

(PAUL *rushes to examine the damage.* ETHEL *crosses to* CATHERINE *and puts an arm round her.*)

ETHEL (*very kindly*). Oh no, dear, you can't go like that.

CATHERINE. Yes, I can. (*She pulls herself away.*) Let me go, please.

(PAUL *goes to the easel.*)

ETHEL. You've got to change your dress, anyhow. And I'm going to make some tea.

CATHERINE. No, thank you, really. (*Suddenly.*) Oh, I'm terribly sorry.

ETHEL. Nothing to be sorry about. Paul was very annoying. Do sit down, dear.

(CATHERINE *sits on the rostrum and* ETHEL *turns to* PAUL, *who is engrossed with his damaged treasure.*)

It's no use fussing about that. (*Going to him.*) You'd better apologize to Catherine while I make some tea.

PAUL. You're not going to make any tea.
ETHEL. I certainly am. We all need some.
PAUL. Then ring for it.
ETHEL. I told you, Mary's out.
PAUL. Ethel, I asked you not to leave——
ETHEL. I can't help that now. Cath needs some tea. Give me that thing. *(She takes the shawl.)* Paul, it really is disgusting.
PAUL. Rubbish!

(She suddenly pushes it into his face.)

(Grinning.) It is a bit high, isn't it?
ETHEL *(to* CATHERINE). Just sit quiet, dear, and take no notice of him. I'll have this thing cleaned before anyone sees it again.
PAUL. Ethel, don't you dare! You'll take all the quality out of it. Ethel, I forbid you——
ETHEL. If there's any more nonsense, it'll go behind the kitchen fire.

(She goes out, closing the door behind her.)

PAUL. My lovely, lovely shawl. Women have no imagination.
CATHERINE. Paul——
PAUL. Must you call me Paul?
CATHERINE. I can't help it. I think of you as Paul.
PAUL. Then you must certainly call my wife "Ethel." She won't mind.
CATHERINE. I won't. It's beastly enough pretending to be friendly. She must be a damn hypocrite being nice to me.
PAUL *(busy cleaning his brushes, etc.).* If there's one thing Ethel isn't, it's a hypocrite. She undoubtedly *feels* like being nice to you.
CATHERINE. Did you tell her not to leave us alone?
PAUL. I did.
CATHERINE. Did you tell her why?
PAUL *(still busy with his brushes).* There wasn't any need.
CATHERINE *(suddenly drooping).* I wish I was dead. *(For a moment she looks quite old with suffering. Then she rises and goes up towards the door, speaking quietly.)* I'm going home. I'll go and change my dress.
PAUL. Good.

*(*CATHERINE *suddenly turns and moves* C. *in desperation.)*

CATHERINE. Paul, what *is* it? What have I done? I'm terribly sorry about the shawl, but you changed to me last week—before you bought it. What is it—*please*? I'll go mad if you don't tell me.
PAUL (R.C.—*irritably).* My dear child——
CATHERINE. Have I done something? I've thought and thought —right through the nights. Oh, it's been so awful—I can't even cry because of Ann hearing. Is it just that you're tired of me—just in a few weeks?

PAUL. For the Lord's sake, shut up, Catherine. You're talking as if—as if something—— Damn it, I haven't even kissed you. Or have I?

CATHERINE. No. You were going to when that wretched old tramp came along.

PAUL (*brushes in hand*). God bless him!

CATHERINE. Paul—that morning on Primrose Hill, when it was all beginning——

PAUL. "It was all beginning."? Well, it isn't going to begin, Catherine. It isn't going on, anyhow.

CATHERINE. But *why*? What's gone wrong? It's not knowing that that's so——

PAUL. Good lord, child, it's pretty obvious. Your father——

CATHERINE. So that's it. Just because you know Father.

PAUL. It isn't all of it. I'm twenty years older—more than twenty years. And—though I hate to stress the fact—I really am married.

CATHERINE. I'm sorry about your wife. But she must be used to it by now. Oh, I know you make love to dozens of people. It's hateful—but it doesn't seem to make any difference.

PAUL (*amused*). I was afraid it mightn't. (*He goes to the paint table.*)

CATHERINE. Don't you care for me at all?

PAUL (*over-doing determination*). No. (*He gets another brush.*)

CATHERINE. I don't believe you. You're just trying to cure me. That day on Primrose Hill——

PAUL. In my whole life I have only once been on Primrose Hill at seven in the morning and you had to be there.

CATHERINE (*intensely*). Don't you think that was Fate?

PAUL. I do not. I think it was the after effects of a studio party in Camden Town.

CATHERINE. Do you mean you were drunk?

PAUL. Certainly not. I am never drunk.—You see, someone at the party said that you could see the Crystal Palace from Primrose Hill—or you couldn't see it—I forget which. So on the way home I thought I'd go and find out.

CATHERINE. Oh, don't keep spoiling it. It was so marvellous. Do you remember——

PAUL. If you want to know, Catherine, I remember remarkably little about it. I don't even remember if you could see the Crystal Palace. (*He puts the brushes back on the paint table.*)

CATHERINE. Oh, do stop about the wretched Crystal Palace!—I'd been in love with you for weeks—but I wouldn't have said anything ever—I knew I'd got to fight it—and then, suddenly, just when I was thinking of you—— (*She stops, a light comes into her eyes.*) Paul, you're just pretending. You couldn't have said those things if you didn't mean them. You're just trying to put me off, for my own good——

D

PAUL. Catherine—for Heaven's sake——
CATHERINE. It's wonderful of you, but it's no good. I can fight now I know I've got something to fight for! (*Gripping his lapels*). Paul, look at me. (*She goes close up to him and looks in his eyes.*)
PAUL (*backing*). You go away.
CATHERINE (*putting her hands on his shoulders and looking up into his face*). I'll never go away.
PAUL. Oh, my sweet child—— (*His arms go round her.*)
(*The door bell rings.* PAUL *breaks away down* R.)
Thank God. (*He mops his forehead.*)
CATHERINE. It was only the door bell.
PAUL. It spoke with the tongue of men and angels. (*Seeing that she is advancing towards him, he waves his hands at her as if scaring her off.*) Tch, tch, tch—Ethel will be back in a minute.
CATHERINE. I'm not ashamed. I'll tell Ethel if you like.
PAUL. You'll do no such thing. Coming in here and rushing at me! Lord, you are a violent girl.
CATHERINE. Tilly Marchmont was a violent girl, wasn't she?
PAUL. Yes, she was, very violent.
CATHERINE. And she got what she wanted, didn't she?
PAUL. Yes—no. (*Pushing her* L.) Here, you keep off there. (*He crosses with her.*) Hard-boiled, that's what you are.
CATHERINE. You can tease me now. It doesn't matter, now that I know. (*She sits on the model's throne.*)
PAUL (*rashly coming towards her*). Now, Catherine, listen——
(CATHERINE *turns quickly, half rises and kneels in the chair, swiftly slipping her arm round his neck.*)
Don't you dare——
(ETHEL's *voice is heard outside saying :*)
ETHEL. Mind that last little step.
(CATHERINE's *arm drops.* PAUL *dashes away from her to* R. ETHEL *enters with the tea-tray, followed by* ANN, *who carries a plate of bread and butter.*)
We've a visitor. (*She crosses to the settee* R. *and puts the tea on the small table.*)
CATHERINE. Ann!
ETHEL. You know Ann, don't you, Paul?
(ANN *puts the plate of bread and butter on the tea-table.*)
ANN (C., *holding out a hand*). We only met for a minute. I don't think you noticed me much.
PAUL (R. *of her, shaking hands*). That was very remiss of me. Come and sit down. (*He places the armchair from up* R. *for her, up* L. *of the tea-table.*)

Sc. 1.]   CALL IT A DAY.   51

(ETHEL *has seated herself on the settee and is pouring out tea.*)
CATHERINE. What do you want?
ANN. Well, as a matter of fact, I want some money. (*She sits in the armchair.*)
PAUL (*his hand in his pocket*). How much?
ANN. Oh no, please—Cath's sure to have it. (*With a sudden rush.*) You see—coming home I saw a little Rossetti print—it's one I've never seen before, a girl with jewels and a hair-brush and an oak frame. It's only four-and-six and the man said it was the last—and it might be gone to-morrow, so I thought as it's nearer to here than to home and I didn't think Mr. Francis would mind as it's all for art—— (*She pauses for breath.*)
PAUL. Have some tea. (*He hands her a cup from the table.*)
ANN. Oh, thank you. You don't mind my coming, do you? I didn't interrupt anything?
PAUL (*who is now handing tea to* CATHERINE *and receiving an ardent look from her*). Oh, no—nothing whatever. (*He returns to get bread and butter.*)
ANN. Could you manage the four-and-six, Cath?
CATHERINE. Oh, I expect so. Heaven knows you've got enough pictures.
ANN. But this is something special.

(PAUL *hands bread and butter to* CATHERINE, *then* ANN, *then* ETHEL.)

Thank you. (*She sits juggling perilously with tea and bread and butter.*) Are you familiar with the works of Dante Gabriel Rossetti, Mr. Francis?
PAUL (*on the upstage arm of the settee, catching her tone*). Tolerably, Miss Hilton—though I don't seem to remember the one you describe. A woman with a hair-brush——
ANN. And a jewel-box, and a monkey and a little glass house and the back view of a peacock.
PAUL (*putting the plate on the tray*). It seems reasonable for four-and-six. An oak frame, I think you said?
ANN. Yes. With a wavy edge.
PAUL. I should snap it up. It's a bargain.
ANN. Could I have the four-and-six reasonably soon, Cath?
ETHEL. More tea, Cath?
CATHERINE. No thanks.
ETHEL. Then you'd better go and change your dress. I'm going to make you run along with Ann. You're too tired to sit any more.
CATHERINE (*rising and taking her cup to the tea-table*). But I'm not a bit tired. I want to sit.
PAUL (*cheerfully*). No. (*Moving up stage.*) Shop's shut for to-day. (*Looking at the painting.*) This thing's all wrong. Not at all sure I shall go on with it.
CATHERINE (*involuntarily, aghast*). Paul! (*She goes to the easel.*)

(PAUL *looks annoyed. There is no reaction from* ETHEL.)

PAUL. Perhaps I shall paint Ann instead. She's got a very interesting mouth.

ANN (*with satisfaction*). Rather morbid, isn't it?

PAUL (*chuckling*). Morbid to a degree. (*To* CATHERINE.) Run and get your bonnet on, young woman.

ETHEL (*rising and crossing up* L.). I expect you'd like a wash, after that horrid shawl. I'll show you.

(CATHERINE *shoots a glance at* PAUL *and then goes out with* ETHEL. ANN *goes and sits on the settee.*)

PAUL (*offering the plate*). More bread and butter?

ANN. Thank you.

(*They both eat thin bread and butter,* PAUL *putting three pieces together.*)

PAUL. Why are three pieces of thin bread and butter nicer than one piece of thick? (*He sits in the chair just vacated by* ANN.)

ANN. You get more butter.

PAUL. True. I perceive you have a fine, logical mind.

ANN. Oh no, not really. Can I have a look at Cath?

PAUL (*rising and going to the easel*). I await your judgment with trepidation.

(ANN *rises, goes up to the easel and looks at the portrait quietly.*) You don't think it's like her?

ANN. No. But it's like what she is.

PAUL (*looking at her, suddenly impressed*). Go on. (*He moves down and round* R. *of the tea-table to* L.)

ANN. I don't understand it very well—all those little dabs. It looks as if—as if you were angry with it.

PAUL (*giving a short laugh*). Ha! Come away from it, you horribly perspicacious child. (*He is* L. *of the easel.*)

ANN. I'm sorry. I don't understand modern art yet—Picasso and Matisse and people. Miss Fry says I'll get to like them.—I liked that one of yours at the Tate, though—the girl in green, wicked-looking.

PAUL. She wasn't very wicked.

ANN (*moving* L.). Could I see some more of your pictures?

PAUL. There's hardly a thing of mine here.

ANN. I expect they all get bought. (*She wanders round.*) You know, this isn't a bit how I imagined your studio.

PAUL. What did you expect—blue china and poppy-heads?

ANN. Oh, no—not arty crafty. But large and white and empty.

PAUL (*with a mock shiver*). I know the places. This was my Dad's studio. It's a good place to paint in.

ANN. There's a little picture of his at the Tate.

PAUL. I know. A girl with some goldfish in a conservatory. They've shoved it away in a corner.

ANN. It's nice. You can almost feel you're in it. Do you know what I mean?

PAUL (*nodding*). Atmospheric. He had a good trick with the light. That's one of his. (*He points to the small picture* L. *of the window.*) It's the view from this window.

ANN (*crossing to the window*). So it is.

(PAUL *opens the window so that she can look out.*) There's that tree coming out. It hasn't changed much. Oh—that big building's new.

PAUL. Yes, damn it.

(ANN *returns to her wanderings round the studio.* PAUL *stands by the window, conscious of the spring air that has invaded the room, and charmed by the little girl's eager, serious air.*)

ANN (*crossing* R.). What lots of fascinating things. (*She stops suddenly.*) Mr. Francis!

PAUL. Yes?

ANN (*at the bookcase up* R., *alight with excitement*). This little one —it isn't—oh, it couldn't be—it's *not a Rossetti*?

PAUL. Yes, by Jove, it is. I'd forgotten all about it. He gave it to my Dad. (*He takes it from the bookcase and sets it on the table down* R.C. *in a better light.*)

ANN (*above the table*). It's lovely. It's not finished, is it?

PAUL (*sitting on the* R. *arm of the chair* C.). No, it's a sketch. You're a clever girl to spot that as his work.

ANN. He must have touched it, mustn't he?

PAUL. He certainly must.

(*She gazes reverently at it while he watches her.*)

(*Suddenly.*) Like to have it?

ANN. Oh, you couldn't—it's not possible—you don't mean——

PAUL. Yes, I do. It's for you.

ANN. But I couldn't—it's frightfully valuable.

PAUL. Not so very. And I should never sell it.

ANN. It's marvellous of you, but—I mustn't, really. It belonged to your father.

PAUL. My Dad would have liked you to have it. He loved Rossetti.

ANN (*taking it—the glory dawning on her*). Oh! Oh, Mr. Francis!

PAUL. Oh, Miss Hilton!

ANN. Please don't call me that. I'm just Ann.

PAUL (*rising*). Then you must call me Paul.

ANN. Really?

PAUL. Really. Yes, I think it would be a very good idea if you called me Paul.

(ETHEL *and* CATHERINE *return,* CATHERINE *now in her ordinary clothes.*)

ANN (*rushing at them*). Look what he's done. He's given me a Rossetti—a real one! I can't believe it. Look!

(*The positions are:* PAUL R. *by the settee;* ANN *upstage slightly* L. *of* C., *with* CATHERINE *on her* R. *and* ETHEL *on her* L.)

CATHERINE (*to* PAUL). Is it real?

(PAUL *nods.*)

You can't possibly take it, Ann.. Mother wouldn't let you.

ANN. Oh, golly—I never thought of that. It's not like money, is it?

ETHEL. Of course it isn't.

PAUL. Don't you worry. I'll square your mother.

CATHERINE. Ann, you've no right——

PAUL. You shut up. I'll settle it, Ann. I *promise* you.

ANN. Oh, thank you. I'm sure you can manage it. Oh, goodness, I must get it home safely. I'll take a taxi instead of buying that picture in the High Street—I don't want it now. You'll lend me the money, won't you, Cath?

ETHEL. I'll get you a piece of flannel to wrap it in and we'll send Mary for the taxi.

(*She goes out.*)

ANN (*crossing to* PAUL). Oh, thank you. (*She turns.*) Come on, Cath—I want to hang it in my room. I'll write to you, Mr. Francis, I mean Paul, and thank you properly. It's a pity I'm too old to hug you.

PAUL. A thousand pities.

ANN (*crossing up* L.). Come on, Cath.

(*She goes out.*)

CATHERINE (*crossing to him*). Paul—please——

PAUL. Now go away. If Ann's too old to hug me you certainly are. (*He dodges her, goes to the door and calls.*) Got that taxi yet?

(CATHERINE *has followed* PAUL *to the door. He takes her by the shoulders and puts her firmly out.*)

(L. *of the door.*) Out you go, young woman.

(*He closes the door firmly after her and heaves a sigh in which relief and regret are mingled. Then he crosses to the easel and looks at his painting, giving a little chuckle at a memory of* CATHERINE. *Finally he pushes the easel away, lights a cigarette and sits on the window-seat, looking through the open window.* ETHEL *returns.*)

ETHEL. That child's in the seventh heaven. (*She crosses to the settee.*) Rather unusual, isn't she?

PAUL. Who? Catherine?

ETHEL. Oh, no, there's nothing unusual about Catherine, except her looks (*She settles on the settee and resumes her knitting.*)

PAUL. Why the hell did you insist on going out of the room for that tea?
ETHEL. Well, I really thought the poor girl deserved a few minutes with you. You'll have to cope with her sooner or later, you know.
PAUL. You are a damned irritating woman—sitting there knitting.
ETHEL (*stopping knitting*). What do you want me to do? Have hysterics? I used those up the first year we were married.
PAUL. Yes, thank God. (*Suddenly, appealingly.*) Ethel, what am I to do?
ETHEL. You might go away. (*She resumes the knitting.*)
PAUL (*looking at the portrait*). And leave this?
ETHEL. You could finish it later.
PAUL. No. She'll never look quite like she does now.

(*The door bell rings.*)

There's that damn bell.
ETHEL. It's all right. Mary's back.
PAUL. Oh, Lord—I don't know what to do.
ETHEL. What happened to-day?
PAUL. I was firm. As a matter of fact, I was damn brutal. I don't think she'll worry us for a day or two.

(CATHERINE *enters and stands by the door.*)

Oh, my God!
CATHERINE (*painfully overwrought and nervous*). I—we didn't fix about the next sitting. I thought——
PAUL. I'll ring you up. I shan't be painting for a day or two.
CATHERINE. Oh, I see. I—— (*She stands, at a loss.*) I wonder if I left my handkerchief here. It isn't in my bag.
ETHEL (*rising*). Let's have a look. (*She crosses* L. *and looks round about the model's throne.*)
CATHERINE (*down* L.). It doesn't seem to be here. I—one feels so awful without a hanky. One's nose starts to tickle on purpose.
ETHEL (*touched by the girl's pathetic little ruse*). I'll get you a clean one.

(*She goes out.* PAUL *throws a furious glance at* ETHEL'S *retreating back, then looks out of the window, turning his back on* CATHERINE.)

CATHERINE (*going to him*). Paul, please—oh, please listen. I don't want to be a nuisance. I know you're doing everything for the best, but—if you could just make me understand—if you'd talk to me quietly—— It's so terrible not being able to see you alone.

(PAUL *rises and turns.*)

PAUL (*furiously*). I don't *want* to see you alone. (*Looking at her, he suddenly softens.*) Now, my dear, listen——

CATHERINE. There's no time now. Paul—please don't be angry, but—would you meet me once more—on Primrose Hill?
PAUL. I would not.
CATHERINE. Then somewhere else. I'll be going for a walk to-night on the Outer Circle. Won't you meet me?
PAUL. The Outer Circle's three miles round.
CATHERINE. But we could fix a place—say, the Zoo——
PAUL (*suddenly roaring with laughter*). The Zoo would be splendid.
CATHERINE. I know it's not very romantic, but you can't miss it.
PAUL. Do you know the Park Villages—the bridge by the Canal?
CATHERINE (*eagerly*). Yes.
PAUL (*moving* R.). No, damn it—we mustn't.
CATHERINE. Paul, you can't back out now—it's too cruel. Nine o'clock.
PAUL. Nine o'clock. Lord, I'm a lunatic.
CATHERINE. No, you're not. Oh, I'm so happy I could die. (*She sits on the window-seat and looks out of the window.*) Look at that lovely, lovely tree!—(*Rising.*) I'll go now—I won't wait for the handkerchief——

(ETHEL *enters.*)

ETHEL. Here you are. (*She holds out the handkerchief.*)
CATHERINE. Oh, thank you. I'll rush now. Ring me up when you want me. Good-bye! Good-bye—Mr. Francis.

(*She runs off.* ETHEL *instantly notices the rather histrionic* " Mr. Francis," *also the girl's exalted manner. She crosses to the settee, sits and picks up her knitting.* PAUL *becomes artificially busy with brushes, etc., whistling a little.*)

ETHEL (*quietly, after a pause*). Are you going to seduce that girl?
PAUL. Really, Ethel!
ETHEL. Because I don't think her parents will like it.
PAUL (*moving down* C.—*furious*). Then why don't they look after her? Why don't you look after her? Dashing out of the room——
ETHEL. What happened?

(PAUL *returns to the window and sits on the window-seat, looking at the tree. Suddenly his expression becomes both impish and mulish.*)

PAUL. You can mind your own business.
ETHEL. I see. It's like that. I was afraid it would be, sooner or later.

(PAUL *rises and moves round the studio, doing various odd jobs, whistling airily.*)

(*In her even quiet voice.*) She's not nineteen yet. Only four years older than the child you gave the picture to.
PAUL (*putting a picture to replace the Rossetti*). Damn it, I'm only going to have a talk to her.

ETHEL. I wonder if Roger Hilton will find out. I should think she's too excitable to be discreet.
PAUL. Of all the infuriating women——
ETHEL (*suddenly*). Paul——
PAUL. What?
ETHEL. I saw Tilly Marchmont last week.
PAUL (*down* c.). You said she was dead.
ETHEL. No, I didn't—you did. She's not dead at all. She's lovelier than ever.
PAUL. Thinner or fatter?
ETHEL. Thinner.
PAUL (*moving up* c.). That's queer. I thought she'd get fat.
ETHEL. She's improved a lot. She was just going out to Majorca. We've never been there.
PAUL (*cleaning the palette*). Fancy old Tilly getting thinner.— Same lovely pudding-face?
ETHEL. She's got more expression. (*There is a pause, while she knits.*) The Edgar Smithsons were in Majorca last year. We could go and talk to them about it this evening.
PAUL (*at the window*). No, not this evening. (*He suddenly looks at* ETHEL.) At least——

(ETHEL *raises her eyes and meets his glance.*)

I'll let you know. (*He drops the palette and knife on the paint table and sits on the window-seat, looking out.*) Think you're clever, don't you?
ETHEL (*knitting again*). I wonder if Cath will let me have that handkerchief back. It was rather a nice one.

CURTAIN.

SCENE 2

SCENE.—FRANK HAINES'S *Sitting-room in a house in Jermyn Street.* 5.15 *p.m.*
It is a pleasant, rather attic-like little room. There are two windows at the back, with window-boxes in which daffodils are growing. The door is R. *There is a table* c. *laid for afternoon tea, with a sofa* R. *of the table and an armchair* L. *of the table. The furniture is semi-antique, in the manner of typical rather old-fashioned service suites.*
(*See Photograph of Scene.*)

When the CURTAIN *rises, the door is opened by* MURIEL WESTON, *a pretty but over-plump woman of about forty, possessed of tremendous conversational vitality. She carries various parcels. Immediately behind her is* DOROTHY, *who is also carrying trophies of a day's shopping.*

MURIEL (*panting*). Isn't this the world's worst climb? (*She flops on the sofa.*) My dear, I'm dead.

DOROTHY (*slightly out of breath*). Well, it's rather nice when you get here. (*She crosses and puts her parcels on the table* L.C.)

MURIEL. Do you think so? It gives me the willies. Can't think why Frank doesn't go to a decent hotel. (*She puts her parcels beside her on the sofa.*)

DOROTHY. How long is it since he was home last?

MURIEL. Let's see—a good five years. Of course, he ought to have got out of rubber when George did.

DOROTHY. Why didn't he?

MURIEL. Oh, I don't know. I really believe he likes the life out there. (*She takes out a large floppy powder-puff and does her face.*)

(DOROTHY *looks at herself in the mirror* L., *takes off her hat and puts it on top of the chest.*)

DOROTHY (*patting her hair*). I don't think she set this as well as usual, do you?

MURIEL. Looks all right to me. (*She takes her hat off.*) My perm's on its last legs.

DOROTHY (*moving* C.). It must be rather marvellous for your brother coming back to England after five years. Everything must look so fresh and exciting.

MURIEL. That's the way he talks. It always looked exactly the same to me. You and Frank'll get along like a house on fire.

DOROTHY (*sitting in the armchair* L.C.). Are you sure he won't mind me coming to-day?

MURIEL. Don't be an ass, my dear. He's lapping it up. Didn't the old lady tell you he rushed out for more cakes as soon as I telephoned.

DOROTHY. And just look at them all ready! I told you we oughtn't to have had that matinée tea.

MURIEL. I know. But my tongue always starts to hang out as soon as those little trays go round. My dear, shall I ever forget it when ours went over! You wouldn't think one tray *could* make such a noise. (*She takes a sandwich from the table.*)

DOROTHY. You certainly wouldn't.

MURIEL. That girl Gwynne glared at me right across the footlights. Jolly inartistic of her in the middle of a tragic scene.

DOROTHY. I really don't blame her.

MURIEL. Well, damn it, we'd paid for our seats. That's how she gets her bread-and-butter, isn't it?

DOROTHY. She got our whole tea-tray.

MURIEL (*taking another sandwich*). Mind you, I think she's good. I bet she's a bit of a witch, though.

DOROTHY. Roger's looking after her income tax.

MURIEL. You keep your eye on him. He might find himself looking after her income.

DOROTHY. Oh, my dear—it takes him all his time to look after ours.
MURIEL. You ought to be married to George for a bit. I wouldn't trust him in the same theatre with that Gwynne girl.
DOROTHY. Doesn't it worry you, Muriel?
MURIEL. Oh, I got used to it out East. You can't really blame a man there—what with the life and the climate. I keep telling him he's in England now, but he says his reactions are still tropical.
DOROTHY. I wonder how I'd feel if Roger——
MURIEL. Oh, Roger's a blinking marvel. You know, Dot, I think he's the only man I know who's decent without being dull.
DOROTHY. He's not a bad old thing.
MURIEL. You don't appreciate your luck. Though I sometimes wonder if he's as respectable as he seems.
DOROTHY. What do you mean?
MURIEL. Nothing, my dear. Instinct—not evidence. If I'd any evidence I should keep it to myself. (*She lies back on the sofa with a grunt.*) I wish one could see plays lying down. Throw me another sandwich, will you? My appetite's coming back.
DOROTHY (*rising*). How you can, after all that currant cake! (*She hands the sandwiches.*)
MURIEL (*taking a sandwich*). Eating's always very natural to me. (*Eating.*) You wouldn't think I was reducing, would you?
DOROTHY (*replacing the sandwiches*). You certainly wouldn't. (*She sits in the armchair again.*)
MURIEL. I'm on a marvellous new system. You eat as much as you can between meals, so that you never really want a big meal.
DOROTHY. Does it work?
MURIEL. Not on me. I seem to want bigger meals than ever. George says I shall be twenty stone before I'm fifty.
DOROTHY. Roger says I shall have a scraggy old age. Am I really getting skinny?
MURIEL. You do look a bit peaked. Of course, you worry too much.
DOROTHY. Yes, I believe I do. And yet, if anyone asked me I'd say I was a perfectly happy woman.
MURIEL. You damn well ought to be.
DOROTHY. There always seems to be just something weighing on one's mind—if it isn't the children, it's the servants.
MURIEL. There's just one reason I'd like to believe in Hell—and that's to think of servants in it.
DOROTHY. You know, I'm not at all sure of this new girl. I believe I'm going to be in for a bad patch. Cook's always been a bit of a menace. Heaven knows I've done all I can to brighten the kitchen—new curtains, pictures——
MURIEL. You're far too good to them.
DOROTHY. Well, after all, they're human beings.
MURIEL. They are not.

DOROTHY. There must be something wrong with the system. I've always felt it's not quite right to be able to pay people to wait on you.

MURIEL. You know, you're going all Bolshie—though I do think it's a pity to have to pay them. I'm all for reviving a spot of slavery. And when you got sick of them you could throw them to the lions.

DOROTHY. Did they throw slaves to lions?

MURIEL. Well, crocodiles, then. Though I shouldn't think a crocodile would stand for my cook. (*She suddenly undoes the straps of her shoes and kicks them off.*)

DOROTHY. You'll never get into those again. (*She picks up a parcel from the table beside her.*)

MURIEL. I know, my dear, but I can't help it. (*She settles back on the sofa, putting a cushion behind her and her feet up.*) Like the sofa for a bit?

DOROTHY. No, thanks. (*She is taking some silk from a paper carrier-bag.*) You know, I'm not a bit sure about this crêpe-de-chine. It's much too strong a pink.

MURIEL. It'll wash out.

DOROTHY. It never does if you want it to. Why is it things look so different out of the shop?

MURIEL. It does look a bit like tinned salmon, doesn't it? Where's my red stuff? (*She picks up a parcel.*)

DOROTHY. That was a marvellous colour.

MURIEL (*having torn a hole in the paper to look through*). Look at it, my dear—bright puce.

DOROTHY (*looking*). Muriel! Have we gone colour blind or something?

MURIEL. It's these girls in the shops. They just dither you. (*She has pulled the silk out of the parcel.*) What am I going to look like? Cardinal Wolsey.

DOROTHY. Wasn't it to wear under your last year's coat?

MURIEL. Well, *that's* out of the question.

DOROTHY. It's always the same when one tries to use up last year's clothes. Wouldn't it be marvellous to start absolutely fresh?

MURIEL. Heavenly. I should like to be naked with a cheque-book. (*Resignedly.*) Oh, hell!

DOROTHY. I wonder if I could use it for Cath? It would suit her.

MURIEL. Dorothy, if you could——! (*She throws the silk to* DOROTHY.)

DOROTHY. Seven-and-eleven a yard, wasn't it?

MURIEL. Eight-and-eleven—here's the bill. (*She opens it, sees it was seven-and-eleven and crumples it up.*) Oh, well, let's say seven-and-eleven.

DOROTHY (*handling it*). It's a bit thin.

MURIEL (*instinctively the saleswoman*). But it's all pure silk—Well, look here—seven-and-six. It's a bargain at that!

DOROTHY *(throwing the silk back)*. I'll have to ask Cath—she doesn't like things being decided for her. I'd better have a pattern
MURIEL *(folding the silk)*. Scissors, scissors—I wonder if old stickin-the-mud's got any scissors. Try those drawers, there.

(DOROTHY *goes to the bureau up* C. *and opens the top drawer*.)

DOROTHY. None there. *(She suddenly notices a photograph on the bureau.)* Muriel—this isn't you ?

MURIEL. Let's have a look.

(DOROTHY *moves down and hands her the photograph*.)

My God, would you think any man would willingly expose that ? This was before I was married.

DOROTHY. Just look at your hobble skirt. That's not George, is it ?

MURIEL. George never looked as pure as that. That's Frank.

DOROTHY. He's not a bit like you.

MURIEL. Are you sure you never met him ?

DOROTHY. Certain.

MURIEL *(looking at the photograph)*. This takes you back a bit, doesn't it ?

DOROTHY *(taking the photograph)*. Look at your superb waistline.

MURIEL. And was it agony ? I'll say so. I don't think anyone'll ever make a waist big enough for me. *(She undoes the top of her skirt.)* You know, Frank's still ridiculously like that.

DOROTHY. He looks nice.

MURIEL. He's a good old thing. We used to be terribly fond of each other when we were kids. But somehow—— I suppose it's because he and George are so unlike.

DOROTHY *(going back to the bureau)*. Aren't Frank's reactions tropical ? *(She replaces the photograph.)*

MURIEL. Good Lord, no. Old Frank's the backbone of the Empire—dresses for dinner each night in his lonely bungalow and thinks women are on a higher plane.

DOROTHY *(moving down again)*. It must be dreadfully lonely for him out there. Why doesn't he marry ?

MURIEL. He's going to, my dear—if I have to drag him to the altar. I'm going to get him all fixed up this leave.

DOROTHY. Does he know ? *(She sits in the armchair.)*

MURIEL. As a matter of fact, he's been a good deal more sensible than I expected. I've been paving the way in my letters for weeks. I think I shall bring it off.

DOROTHY. Who's the girl ?

MURIEL. Dolly Walton.

DOROTHY. Oh ! No one I know.

MURIEL. Of course you know her. She sat next to Roger last time you came to dinner. Fairish—a bit heavy.

DOROTHY. Oh ! I remember. Not very exciting, is she ?

MURIEL. Well, rubber planters can't be choosers. Dolly's not a bad old thing. Of course, she's a bit short in the wind and long in the tooth—but she's still got most of her faculties.
DOROTHY (*laughing*). Muriel, you are revolting.
MURIEL. But, my dear——
DOROTHY. I could understand it if it was some charming young girl you'd found for him——
MURIEL. Good Lord, how am I to get him a charming young girl—sandbag her? He isn't even well-off any more. Besides, he'd be miserable with a young girl. He and Dolly will rub along splendidly.
DOROTHY. Oh, well—if they both really like each other.
MURIEL. Don't be funny—they haven't met yet.
DOROTHY. Oh, good heavens—then the whole thing's just in the air.
MURIEL. It certainly is not. The whole point is that they haven't met. I've fixed up three girls like this. As a matter of fact I've never had a failure.
DOROTHY. What do you mean?
MURIEL. The point is to get the thing so settled in their minds before they meet that neither of them likes to back out. Not that Dolly will be doing any backing out. She's had a new perm and a course of face massage. The old war-horse is going right into battle.
DOROTHY. I never heard anything so cold-blooded. Trying to force your own brother——
MURIEL. Dorothy, don't be such an idiot. It's just a matter of common sense—Frank needs a wife and old Dolly needs a husband—and how she needs one. She'll be thanking God on her knees—if she can still get down on them.
DOROTHY (*laughing*). Muriel, you really are disgusting. I hope he jolly well picks someone for himself.
MURIEL. He won't, my dear. He'll never let old Dolly down. They're both coming to stay at Easter. I'll bet you I get their engagement announced within a week. (*Suddenly looking at her watch.*) I say, it's twenty-five to six. What's happened to the old thing?
DOROTHY. What time's your train?
MURIEL. Six-fifteen. Shall I ask the old woman to make us some tea?
DOROTHY. You don't really want any more?
MURIEL. I do, my dear—I shan't get dinner till eight. How I wish I lived in Town.
DOROTHY. But it's lovely where you are. How's the garden looking?
MURIEL. Oh—gardenish. It costs a hell of a lot.
DOROTHY. It must do. I know over our bit of a cabbage-patch. I wish Martin would take an interest in it. You know, I'm worried

about that boy. He's going into Roger's office after Easter—and they do get on each other's nerves.

MURIEL. Oh, for goodness' sake stop worrying about them. What you want's something really to worry about. It would do you good if Roger was to break out. Though I suppose it would do you more good if you were to break out yourself.

DOROTHY. What do you mean?

MURIEL. Have you ever thought of kicking over the traces?

DOROTHY. No. Have you?

MURIEL. Have I what—thought or kicked? As a matter of fact, I've done both.

DOROTHY. Muriel! Don't you feel awful about it?

MURIEL. I feel damn pleased, when I think of how George goes on. But it's made me understand him better. People make a hell of a fuss over that sort of thing. But it doesn't really mean much.

DOROTHY. I couldn't ever feel like that.

MURIEL. I believe you're shocked.

DOROTHY. Rubbish! But it's rather flabbergasting. Somehow it makes you quite different.

MURIEL. It doesn't really. You try it and see.—I say, I'll have to go. (*She rises and begins to collect herself.*)

DOROTHY. I wish you hadn't told me just as you're dashing off. I'd have liked to have talked about it.

MURIEL. We'll take our back hair down on it one of these days. It's all very ancient history. (*She grunts, struggling into her shoes.*) I shall have to leave these straps undone. (*She puts on her hat.*)

DOROTHY. Muriel——

MURIEL. My dear, you're looking at me as if I was the original scarlet woman—and I shall be if I wear this stuff. (*She picks up the red silk and throws it to* DOROTHY.) Look, take the whole lot and try it on Cath. (*She rises.*) I'll take seven bob a yard—for cash. (*She is gathering up her parcels.*)

DOROTHY. You must just wait till Frank comes.

MURIEL. I can't, my dear. He must have been run over or something.

(FRANK HAINES *enters, carrying some almond blossom done up in paper, a box of cakes and a pot of tea. He is a pleasant-looking man, a little over forty, with a shy, rather boyish manner.*)

Where on earth have you been, you old idiot?

FRANK (*crossing* C. *to above the table*). I'm most frightfully sorry. (*He looks round, trying to get rid of his burdens.*)

DOROTHY (*rising*). Let me take something. (*She takes the teapot and puts it on the table.*)

FRANK. Thanks awfully. I brought it up because the old lady finds the stairs such a strain.—I got stuck in Bond Street—had to get out of the taxi and walk.

(DOROTHY *undoes the cakes.*)

MURIEL. I'm just going. What made you dash out like that?
FRANK. I wanted some more cakes—and some flowers. I thought perhaps one of you—— (*He looks at* DOROTHY.)
MURIEL. My dear, how marvellous. (*She snatches the flowers.*) Almond blossom! There's hell to pay if I take any out of the garden. Thanks ever so much. I've got to fly.
FRANK. But you'll have some tea?
MURIEL. I'll just have a cake. Dot's got loads of time. I don't need to introduce you, do I? My God, my skirt's coming off. Here, hold these.

(FRANK *holds her parcels while she does up her waist-band.*)

Last time I did this the damn thing fell off at Victoria.
FRANK. But I say—do wait a minute.
MURIEL. Can't, my dear. I've simply got to get George's watch. (*Counting her parcels as she takes them back.*) Let's see, soap, gloves, suspenders, stockings, Woolworth's—yes, I'm all set. Just pile the flowers on top, will you?

(FRANK *does so.*)

And I'll get the old dame to call me a hearse.
FRANK. You haven't had your cake.
MURIEL. Put it in my mouth.

(FRANK *does so.*)

(*Completely unintelligible with her mouth full.*) Good-bye, Dot, old dear. See you Easter, Frank.

(*She hurries out.*)

FRANK (*who has followed her across*). What?
DOROTHY. I think she said she'd see you at Easter.
FRANK (*closing the door after* MURIEL). Oh yes, of course—Easter. It's only a week. (*Moving to* L. *of the sofa.*) I've been looking forward to it.
DOROTHY. I think everyone likes Easter.—(*Sitting in the armchair.*) Shall I pour out for you?
FRANK. Oh yes, please.
DOROTHY. It's a superb tea. I never saw such lovely cakes.
FRANK. The blossom—I meant—it was really for you.
DOROTHY. For me? How nice of you. Sugar?
FRANK (*sitting at* L. *end of the sofa*). Two lumps.
DOROTHY. So do I. We're neither of us afraid of getting fat.

(*She passes him his tea. She is obviously trying to set him at his ease.*)

FRANK. No. It's funny, that. In that snapshot I saw of you, you looked—well, much fatter. You haven't been ill, have you?

DOROTHY. Heavens, no. Snapshots are terrible things. I look dreadful in them.
FRANK. You do look—different. (*Passing the cakes.*) I say, do have a cake. I know from Muriel you like chocolate ones.
DOROTHY (*taking one*). Did she tell you that on the 'phone? I expect it's because she likes them herself.
FRANK. Isn't she a greedy old darling? (*He helps himself to a cake.*) Once, when we were kids, she ate two-shillingsworth of ice-cream out of penny cones.
DOROTHY. I believe she could do it now.
(*They laugh together. Both are getting on with their tea.*)
Isn't it funny we've never met? I believe we have, though.
FRANK. Oh, no, I shouldn't have forgotten. What makes you think so?
DOROTHY. It's just—somehow, I feel as if I know you.
FRANK. I feel that too. It's good, isn't it? I thought I was going to be so dreadfully self-conscious.
DOROTHY (*laughing*). Did you?
FRANK. Of course, Muriel's a wonderful woman, but she's—— well, not very imaginative. Just throwing us together like this —it might have been so awkward.
DOROTHY. Might it? Why?
FRANK. We mightn't have liked each other.
DOROTHY. Well, that wouldn't have been very serious.
FRANK. It would to me. (*Offering the box.*) I say, have another cake.
DOROTHY. No, really—I couldn't. I shall have to go soon.
FRANK. Oh, please don't. I was wondering—are you fond of theatres?
DOROTHY. Very. Muriel and I have just done a matinée—a play called " Swift Contact."
FRANK. Was it good?
DOROTHY. Oh, middling. Not very convincing—two people meeting for the first time and rushing into violent love. It never happens, really.
FRANK. I think it might in certain circumstances.
DOROTHY. They'd have to be very queer ones. More tea?
FRANK. No, thanks. I say—I don't suppose you feel like another theatre, but—couldn't we have dinner?
DOROTHY. That's awfully nice of you, but I've got to get back.
FRANK. Oh—I'm sorry.
DOROTHY. I expect you're finding it a bit lonely until you go down to Muriel. I wish you'd come along and see us.
FRANK. I'd love to. I'd no idea you were staying in Town. (*He reaches for the cake box, but knocks it on to the floor. He picks it up.*) I'm making an awful fool of myself. I'm not always like this. I—I think it must be relief.

DOROTHY. What on earth do you mean?
FRANK. I suppose I'd better make a clean breast of it. When old Muriel rang me up after lunch I—I almost felt like dashing under a bus—I say, you didn't loathe me on sight, did you?
DOROTHY. Good heavens, no.
FRANK. Of course, it's too much to hope you feel like I do—as relieved, I mean. But then perhaps you weren't feeling so bad. And then it's so easy for a woman—you can always back out.
DOROTHY (rising). Back out?
FRANK (also rising). Oh, for God's sake don't think *I* want to back out. The minute I saw you—— Don't quell me, I think I've gone a little mad.
DOROTHY (flabbergasted, but laughing). I think you have.
FRANK. It's the relief, I tell you. All afternoon you've been getting fatter and fatter and older and older—and, damn it, you're the prettiest woman I've ever seen in my life. Let's shake hands, shall we? We haven't yet. (*He takes her hand.*)
DOROTHY (protesting). Mr. Haines——
FRANK. Oh, come—— (*He is shaking her hand violently.*)
DOROTHY. Well, Frank, then—please——
FRANK. Am I allowed to call you Dolly yet?
DOROTHY. No one ever calls me Dolly.
FRANK. Muriel does.
DOROTHY. No—Dot or Dorothy. (*Dropping into the armchair.*) Oh! (*She suddenly realizes what has happened.*)
FRANK. Well, I shall call you Dolly. I say, you're looking terribly frigid. I won't try to rush you any more. I suppose you wanted us to meet just as casual acquaintances, but somehow—well, it seems so damn hypocritical after Muriel's letters—and I wanted us to be friends as soon as possible.

(DOROTHY *rises and crosses* R. *below the sofa.*)

Have I offended you?
DOROTHY (terribly distressed). Oh, it isn't that.
FRANK (crossing to her). I've been all sorts of a damn fool. You're sensitive about the whole thing. I'll tell you what—let's drop it now, and to-morrow I'll hire a car—we'll go out in the country. I'm sure we can get it straight if——
DOROTHY. Oh, stop—stop! I'm Dorothy Hilton—not Dorothy Walton.
FRANK (quietly). Oh, my God!
DOROTHY. I've got a husband and grown-up children.—I kept trying to stop you.

(FRANK *turns away and goes to the window* L.C. *She watches him. There is a moment's dead silence. Then he turns to her.*)

(*Crossing to him at the desk.*) I'm so terribly sorry.

FRANK. I can't even start to apologize.
DOROTHY. It's my fault. I was so slow. It was quite a natural mistake—Dot Hilton, Dolly Walton—on the telephone——
FRANK. Yes. Please don't let it worry you.
DOROTHY (*pretending to be casual*). Fancy us talking at cross purposes. (*Crossing down* R.) Of course, Dolly's a great friend of Muriel's—naturally you'd ask her out.
FRANK. You know all about Dolly?
DOROTHY. No, I don't.—Oh, Muriel just said she hoped you'd be friends—naturally, you need someone to go about with while you're home.
FRANK (*going to her*). Sit down a minute, please.
DOROTHY. I've really got to go.
(FRANK *looks straight at her. She goes to the armchair and sits.*)
FRANK (*moving to* L. *of the table*). I know you think it's kinder to ignore what's happened—to pretend I haven't made a god-dam fool of myself—but it doesn't work like that on me. You see, nothing like this has ever happened to me. I ought to want to shoot myself. But I don't.
DOROTHY (*brightly*). Of course you don't.
FRANK. I say, do stop trying to pass the whole thing off as if it didn't mean anything.
DOROTHY. But what *am* I to do?
FRANK. Just listen to me. (*He sits at* L. *end of the sofa.*) I'm in love with you.
DOROTHY (*gently*). It's nonsense, you know—it's just because you've been planning to fall in love—because you've been lonely.
FRANK. I daresay. It doesn't make any difference, though. Do you like me at all?
DOROTHY. Of course I do. You're Muriel's brother.
FRANK. Oh, cut that out.
DOROTHY. Well, I like you anyhow—we could have been friends.
FRANK. Then let's be friends. Are you happily married?
DOROTHY. Yes.
FRANK. Because if not——
DOROTHY. But I am, I tell you.
FRANK. All right. I'll come and see. I won't be a nuisance. Half a loaf, you know.
DOROTHY. But there isn't even half a loaf.
FRANK. Then crumbs, my dear. I'll be grateful for anything I can get. When can I come?
DOROTHY (*pulling herself together*). This is insane. Of course you can't come. You must go down to Muriel's and meet Dolly.
FRANK. Dolly. Have you seen Dolly?
DOROTHY. Yes.
FRANK. Is she fat?
DOROTHY. No—not very.

FRANK. I bet she is. She's probably worse than the snapshot. Got a face like the back of a cab.

DOROTHY. No, really. She *is* a bit like me, only—a bit heavier.

FRANK. Can I come this evening?

DOROTHY. No.

FRANK. To see the grown-up children and the happy husband, damn him?

DOROTHY. Look here——

FRANK. Don't you see that I'm not normal? Any normal man would be grovelling with embarrassment, longing for you to go.

DOROTHY (*rising*). I'm going, anyhow.

FRANK (*rising*). Suppose I insist on kissing you?

DOROTHY. I know what it is. You're like Muriel's husband— your reactions are still tropical. (*She goes* L.)

FRANK. I tell you I never *had* any reactions before. You've got a boy to cope with.

DOROTHY. I've got a lunatic to cope with. (*Her manner suddenly changes.*) Look here, are you talking all this nonsense to put me at my ease—to make me feel that this wretched mistake—that you don't mind.

FRANK. But I mind like hell.

DOROTHY. I'm desperately sorry—but what can I do?

FRANK. Let me come and see you—let me work this thing out my own way. Where do you live?

DOROTHY. Forty-six Beech Tree Road—it's off St. John's Wood Road. Oh, but you mustn't—anyhow, not till you've seen Dolly.

FRANK. To hell with Dolly! The whole thing was insane.

DOROTHY. Oh, poor Dolly! She had a new perm. (*She starts to laugh.*)

FRANK. A what?

DOROTHY (*crossing* R.—*through her laughter*). I know it's awful, but I can't stop laughing.

(FRANK *has also started to laugh. Still laughing, he strolls round by the windows. His eye falls on the window-boxes up* L.C.)

FRANK. Damn it, you shall have some flowers. (*He opens the window and plucks the daffodils.*)

DOROTHY. Oh, no—not your daffodils—oh, please don't.

(*Through the open window comes the sound of a clock striking six.*)

There's six o'clock striking. (*Moving* C.) I'm going. (*She collects her parcels feverishly.*)

FRANK (*placing the flowers on her arm*). There. I'm coming this evening at nine oclock.

DOROTHY. No—really—oh, where's my hat——

(FRANK *finds her hat on the chest* L. *and puts it on her head where it looks ridiculous.*)

We've both gone crazy—I'll think about it—I'll write to you——
(*For a second she looks at him, then crushes her hat on somehow and, clutching parcels and flowers, dashes from the room.*)

FRANK (*following her to the door and calling after her*). Forty-six Beech Tree Road—this evening. At nine o'clock.

CURTAIN.

SCENE 3

SCENE.—ROGER HILTON'S *Office in the Temple.* 5.55 *p.m.*
It is a first-floor room, overlooking an old court. The windows are in the back wall and have old wooden window-seats and shutters. The room has been an office for generations, but it still retains a certain charm.

Deed-boxes are stacked on shelves and there is the usual paraphernalia of framed certificates and a faded photograph or two on the walls. ROGER'S *desk and chair stand* R., *a chair facing them. There is a small bowl of very bright scillas on the desk.*

(*See Photograph of Scene.*)

When the CURTAIN *rises,* ROGER *is at his desk signing letters.* ELSIE LESTER, *a neat, anæmic girl of twenty-seven, is standing by him.*

ROGER (*looking up from a letter*). Who's F. L. C. ?

ELSIE (*above* ROGER). Miss Crampton. I've been using her while Mr. Hedges is in Paris.

ROGER. Not fussy about spelling, is she ?

ELSIE (*leaning over to see the mistake*). I think I can alter that.

ROGER (*signing*). Hedges is a lucky devil. Paris in spring. He gets all the dashing clients. I get all the duds.

ELSIE. Oh, Mr. Hilton ! All the firm's most important clients are yours.

ROGER. All the stodgy ones. None of them ever ask me to chase over to Paris after them.

ELSIE. I've never been to Paris.

ROGER. I had Paris leave once in spring. All the chestnuts were out.

ELSIE. It's funny—everyone talks about the chestnuts in Paris, never in London.

ROGER (*busy with letters*). Are there any in London ?

ELSIE. Oh, Mr. Hilton ! Regent's Park's full of them. I come through the Broad Walk every morning. Of course, they're not out yet.

ROGER. I didn't know you lived that way.

ELSIE. In Albert Road. I've a little room right at the top of the house. It's nice—except for the water.

ROGER. What's wrong with the water ?

ELSIE. You have to go right down five flights for it—the bathroom's in the basement. You'd think they'd have a tap on the stairs, wouldn't you?

ROGER. You certainly would. (*Signing the last letter.*) That the lot?

ELSIE. There's the long one to the Clanradden Colliery. I'll have it finished before you go. (*She gathers up the letters.*)

ROGER. All right. Barge in when it's ready. (*Looking at his watch.*) I say, it's six o'clock. Miss Gwynne's half an hour late.

ELSIE. I don't expect she'll turn up.

ROGER. She'll turn up in Brixton if she doesn't get this settled soon. (*He taps a folder of papers.*)

ELSIE. You'd think she'd have had the decency to telephone.

ROGER. Probably forgotten—she had a matinée. Stage people are always damn casual. Cut along and finish that letter. Don't want you working late on a decent evening like this.

ELSIE. I've got nothing to hurry home for.

ROGER. What do you do with your evenings? Pictures?

ELSIE. No, not often. They're not much fun when you're alone. I walk mostly—round the Park.

ROGER. Alone?

ELSIE. Oh, yes. As a matter of fact, I got rather a fright last night. A man drove up behind me, in the Outer Circle, and leaned out of his car.

ROGER. Did he, by Jove.

ELSIE. And whistled. I felt awful.

ROGER. What happened?

ELSIE. He got quite level with me and *looked* at me. And then he drove on.

ROGER. Phew!

ELSIE. Oh, Mr. Hilton, I believe you're laughing at me.

ROGER. Perish the thought. Look—you get those letters done and then I'll run you home in my car. It's on my way.

ELSIE. Oh, Mr. Hilton—thanks ever so. I——

(*The buzzer rings on* ROGER'S *desk.*)

ROGER (*answering the house telephone*). Yes?—Right, send her up. (*Turning to* ELSIE.) That girl's actually turned up.

ELSIE. Miss Gwynne? What frightful cheek. Oh dear, she'll keep you late.

ROGER. No, she won't. Not if she sticks to the point.

ELSIE. Must I get her some tea?

ROGER. No—she'll gossip if she gets tea. Come in with that letter when it's finished. It'll help to hurry her.

ELSIE (*crossing* L.). Very well, Mr. Hilton. (*She opens the door and then stands back.*) This way, please.

(*She holds the door for* MISS GWYNNE *and then slips out, closing the door behind her.*)

CALL IT A DAY.

(BEATRICE GWYNNE *is a very handsome young woman in the early twenties. Not at all a typical actress, she is more the accepted idea of an art student. She wears a black felt hat, a black cloak and a bright blue dress.*)

ROGER (*rising and crossing* C.). Good afternoon—come and sit down, won't you?

BEATRICE (*shaking hands*). I'm late. I ought to have put you off. (*She sits in the armchair* C. *and puts her bag and gloves on the desk.*)

ROGER. I'm glad you didn't. This is getting urgent. Sir Harold's told us a lot about you.

BEATRICE. Old Harold thinks I'll end in jail.

ROGER. I think we can save you from that. (*He crosses above her to* R.) The Inland Revenue never kills any geese while they can cough up golden eggs. (*Offering the cigarette-box.*) Do you smoke?

BEATRICE. No, thanks. Am I really going to get into trouble?

ROGER (*replacing the cigarette-box*). Not if you pay up. (*He sits* R. *of the desk.*)

BEATRICE. On all that money I made in America?

ROGER. I'm afraid so.

BEATRICE. I can't, you know. I haven't got it.

ROGER. Spent it?

BEATRICE. I suppose so. It's gone.

ROGER. Extravagant young person.

BEATRICE. I say, do you mind cutting out the coy fatherly stuff? I'm feeling irritable.

ROGER. I'm sorry. Like some tea?

BEATRICE. Yes, I would.

ROGER (*on the house telephone*). Send up some tea, will you, please.—I expect you're tired after your matinée.

BEATRICE. Oh, I'm not tired. Just bad-tempered. (*She has been jabbing his desk with the point of a pencil.*) I've broken that.

ROGER (*taking a pencil from a drawer and offering it to her*). Have another.

(BEATRICE *catches his eye and gives a little snort of laughter; then looks irritable again. She pulls off her hat, running her fingers through her hair, then pulls her chair into the desk.*)

BEATRICE. Oh, come on—let's get down to it. What do I have to do?

ROGER. Just answer a few questions to start with.

BEATRICE. They can't really make me pay eight hundred, can they?

ROGER. No. That's just a fictitious demand to force you to make a return. What did you actually earn in the States?

BEATRICE. Nearly two thousand pounds. (*Violently.*) But I tell you I paid income tax on it over there. It's not fair——

ROGER (*calming her*). I know, I know. I'm on your side entirely, but the Government's against us. (*Consulting papers.*) Let's see, that was in nineteen thirty-three. They've been pretty patient, you know.—Well, now. Where were you living in America?

BEATRICE. What on earth's that got to do with you?

ROGER (*bursting into laughter*). I'm not going to ask you another question till you've had your tea. You must have had a wretched matinée. Did they throw things at you?

BEATRICE. Oh, no—they clapped most politely. And the play'll never be heard of again. It's a shame, because it's a damn good play. I persuaded Harold to put it on, you know.

ROGER (*watching her with interest*). Did you?

BEATRICE. I'm sick of his everlasting drawing-room comedies. But it's no good. He can't do anything else now. There was a love scene in this play to-day—a real one, not a flirtation over the tea-cups. One might as well have been playing with a lamp-post.

ROGER. I can't imagine him in a really emotional part.

BEATRICE. As a matter of fact, he wasn't so bad in the beginning—it was just at the opening of the third act. And then a cow of a woman upset a tea-tray in the stalls. After that he went to bits.

ROGER. Pretty disconcerting for you both.

BEATRICE. Everyone giggled and hushed and turned round. It's the first real part I've had since I came back from America. Do you wonder I feel savage?

ROGER. No.

BEATRICE. I've never played a big love scene before. It's the most extraordinary feeling—almost larger than life. And then, suddenly, when Harold went all wooden—— It was like a smack in the face.

ROGER. You'll get other chances, you know.

BEATRICE (*gloomily*). I wonder.

ROGER. I'm sure. We get a good many actresses here. You're right out of the usual run. Fawcett's giving you a contract, isn't he?

BEATRICE. I haven't signed it. And I'm damned if I'm going to.

ROGER. But, my dear girl——

BEATRICE. What good is it to me? Pretty little parts in pretty little plays. God, I am fed up with Harold.

ROGER. He's been pretty good to you, hasn't he?

BEATRICE. Why shouldn't he be? He's in love with me.

ROGER (*embarrassed*). Hm! Well, you'll probably snub me again—but I think you'd better accept that contract.

BEATRICE. Why?

ROGER (*tapping the folder of papers*). Because sooner or later you'll have to settle this thing, and the best way is to give them a proportion of a regular salary.

BEATRICE. But don't you see, I'll be tied up? If I'm free I've a chance of some decent parts. I thought I'd go down to the Key

Theatre for a bit. They can only give me three pounds a week, but——
 ROGER. You can't pay off several hundred pounds out of that.
 BEATRICE. But they can't really want all that. I was out of work six months when I got back——
 ROGER. I know, my child—but it was in the next financial year. It's damned unfair, but there it is.
 BEATRICE. Isn't there anything we can do?
 ROGER. Yes. We can put down every reasonable expense you might have had. And a few unreasonable ones. We'd better start with the American expenses. Now——

(ELSIE *enters with a cup of tea and crosses* R.)

Ah—here's your tea.
 ELSIE (*above the desk*). The sugar's in the saucer. (*She puts the tea on the upstage end of the desk.*)
 BEATRICE. Thank you.

(ELSIE *crosses* L. *and goes out.*)

(*Looking after* ELSIE.) I played one of those once. Is she in love with you?
 ROGER. God forbid!
 BEATRICE. I expect she is. (*She touches the bowl of scillas on his desk.*) Did she put those on your desk?
 ROGER. Yes, but——
 BEATRICE. Then she is.—They can't help it, you know. (*She drinks her tea.*)
 ROGER. Good Lord!
 BEATRICE. What's the matter?
 ROGER. I was just thinking how awful it would be if you were right.
 BEATRICE. Not really. They never get violent. (*She gets up and, still holding her tea-cup, wanders to* C.) I say, this is a nice office. Not a bit what I expected.
 ROGER (*watching her, amused*). Isn't it?
 BEATRICE (*turning and looking at the deed-boxes* R.). Shall I have a box like that?
 ROGER. Well, not to start with. Just a file.
 BEATRICE (*going up* L.C. *and kneeling on the window-seat*). I like this place. Funny to think of work being done here.
 ROGER. Work's been done here for several centuries.
 BEATRICE. Yes, I suppose it has. (*She sits* L. *on the window-seat.*) I didn't know there were any accountants in the Temple—I thought it was all barristers.
 ROGER. It is mostly. We're just a fluke.
 BEATRICE (*rising*). Nice old house. (*Looking at the shutters.*) Do these shutters work?
 ROGER. I haven't the remotest idea.

74   CALL IT A DAY.   [ACT II.

(BEATRICE *tugs at the glass knob of the shutter* R. *of the* L.C. *window. It comes off.*)

BEATRICE (*holding out the knob*). I've broken this.

ROGER (*rising and crossing to her*). Destructive person. (*He takes the knob from her, puts it on the desk and returns to her.*)

BEATRICE (*casually*). Sorry. (*She is gazing out of the window* L.C.)

ROGER. What are you looking at? (*He kneels on the window-seat, following her gaze.*)

BEATRICE. Nothing in particular. (*She turns, so that she is kneeling facing him.*) I like it here. You're not a bit my idea of an accountant.

ROGER. What *is* your idea?

BEATRICE. Old and doddery, like a solicitor.

ROGER (*laughing*). You mean a stage solicitor.

BEATRICE. Do I? Perhaps I do. (*She smiles up into his face.*)

(*For a moment* ROGER *is completely fascinated by her. He looks directly into her eyes.*)

(*Her eyes holding him.*) What exactly *is* an accountant?

ROGER (*pulling himself together*). You come and find out. (*He goes back to his desk and sits.*) Now, let's get down to these expenses. In New York: I suppose you lived in an hotel?

(BEATRICE *leaves her cup on the window-seat, and crosses to the upstage end of the desk.*)

BEATRICE. Only for a bit. I was in a studio most of the time.

ROGER. What was the rent?

BEATRICE (*sitting on the upstage* L. *corner of the desk*). I don't know. I didn't pay it. I wanted to share it, but my young man wouldn't let me. (*She has picked up her hat and is plucking the blue scillas to make a nosegay for it.*)

ROGER. What young man?

BEATRICE (*putting the flowers in the ribbon on her hat*). The young man I was living with. (*She says this with studied nonchalance, but her eyes travel quickly to watch its effect on him.*)

ROGER. Hm! (*Fully aware that she is watching him, he exhibits no surprise whatever.*) Well, I think we'll tell the inspector you paid the rent.

BEATRICE. Oh, please don't bother to whitewash me.

ROGER. My good girl——

BEATRICE. Don't call me your good girl.

ROGER. Not suitable? (*He catches her eye and chuckles.*) Now, look here, Miss Beatrice Gwynne with the flowers in your hat. The inspector doesn't give two hoots who you lived with in America and neither do I, so you can just stop trying to shock me. The inspector wants your money and I want to save it for you, so let's get down to brass tacks and think up some expenses.

Sc. 3.]   CALL IT A DAY.   75

BEATRICE (*holding up her hat with the flowers in it*). Looks nice, doesn't it?
ROGER. Charming. My secretary will be delighted.
BEATRICE. Oh, yes—I'd forgotten her. (*She twiddles the hat on her finger, then puts it on comically and gets off the desk.*) Do you like me?
ROGER. Yes.
BEATRICE. Good. I like you. (*She takes the hat off again.*) I say, I don't feel awfully like concentrating on this stuff. (*She moves down c.*)
ROGER. So I've noticed.
BEATRICE. Why not bring all the papers up to my flat this evening?
ROGER. Am I being invited to come up and see you some time.

(*A moment's pause and then she looks straight at him.*)

BEATRICE. Yes.
ROGER. Are you trying to make a fool of me?
BEATRICE. No. I mean it.
ROGER. Do you know it's exactly ten minutes since we met?
BEATRICE (*crossing and sitting on the desk again*). That's got nothing to do with it. I knew after five minutes—less than that. (*She puts her hat on the desk.*)
ROGER. What, exactly, did you know?
BEATRICE. Do I have to put it into words?
ROGER. No—I don't think you'd better. Do you know what I'm going to do? (*He taps the folder.*) I'm going to hand over all this to one of my partners, a dear old gentleman with long white whiskers. You'll like him. I'm going to make the appointment now, if he hasn't gone. (*He rings on the house telephone.*)

(BEATRICE *watches him closely. There is no answer on the telephone.*)

(*Rising.*) He must have gone. I'll get him to ring you to-morrow. Shall I order you a taxi?
BEATRICE (*a little shaken*). You're not playing fair, you know. You let me see just now that you were—interested.
ROGER. Interested!
BEATRICE. You ought to have snubbed me earlier.
ROGER. Good Lord, I'm not snubbing you. (*Sitting.*) But I really don't know if I'm on my head or my heels. This sort of thing's probably an everyday occurrence with you.
BEATRICE. No, it isn't—not like this.
ROGER. Well, nothing even remotely like it's ever happened to me.
BEATRICE. You might get used to it.
ROGER. I might indeed.
BEATRICE (*rising and moving round above the desk to him*). Let me see what you've written.

ROGER. You haven't given me a chance to write anything.
BEATRICE (*looking down at him*). Are you really going to snub me?
ROGER. Oh, my child—do you realize I'm just a stodgy, middle-aged, married man?
BEATRICE. I don't mind your being married.
ROGER. That's extremely magnanimous of you—but—no, my dear, it won't do. I'll tell you why——

(ELSIE *enters with a letter.*)

ELSIE (*crossing to* L. *of the desk*). Oh, I'm sorry—but the Clanradden Receivership—the letter ought to go off.
ROGER. Right. Leave it, will you? Miss Gwynne will be a few minutes yet.

(ELSIE *puts the letter on the desk and sees* BEATRICE'S *hat with the scillas in it. She gives an involuntary gasp of astonishment, then stalks out.*)

BEATRICE. Poor little rat. I've got a fellow feeling with her now.
ROGER. In Heaven's name, why?
BEATRICE. It looks as if both of us would have to suffer from blighted liyes.
ROGER. Blighted fiddlesticks.
BEATRICE (*picking up her hat*). I'll send you some more flowers for your desk. (*She moves round to* L. *of the desk.*)
ROGER (*rising*). Don't you dare.

(*She picks up her gloves and moves to* L.C. ROGER *takes up her handbag and goes to her with it.*)

What was I saying when she came in?
BEATRICE. You were about to tell me why it—us—my kind invitation—wouldn't do.
ROGER. Was I?
BEATRICE (*looking up at him*). Well, go on. Why won't it do?
ROGER. I've forgotten.
BEATRICE. Are you coming to see me to-night?
ROGER. Yes, damn it, I am. (*He is holding her shoulders.*) And I'll make you give me those figures if I have to shake them out of you. (*He shakes her.*)
BEATRICE. All right. There won't be any secretaries barging in.
ROGER. And no one upsetting trays of tea in the stalls.
BEATRICE (*looking at him sharply*). That's rather clever of you.
ROGER. Oh, I'm not such a fool as I look.
BEATRICE. I wonder if you're right.
ROGER. I'm past wondering anything.
BEATRICE (*crossing down* R.). Nine o'clock?
ROGER (C.). Do you know I've a daughter nearly as old as you?
BEATRICE (*turning to him*). A nice quiet girl, I expect.
ROGER. I wouldn't call her that. Though I can't see her——

Sc. 3.] CALL IT A DAY. 77

BEATRICE (*moving up* R. *of the desk*). Throwing herself at a man? Don't you be too sure. You're behind the times, you know. Nine o'clock?

(ROGER *goes to her. The telephone buzzes.*)

ROGER (*answering it*). All right, bring them up.—My secretary's determined to get you out.

BEATRICE (*at upstage* R. *corner of the desk*). Nine o'clock?

ROGER (*moving up to her*). Look here. I don't think either of us is quite sane.

BEATRICE (*very close to him*). Nine o'clock?

ROGER. Yes.

BEATRICE. Good. (*Crossing to the window* L.C.) We can now compose our expressions for the entrance of Rabbit-face. Don't you think you ought to look a little less intense?

(ROGER *hurriedly looks away from her, sits at the desk and studies his letter.* ELSIE *enters and crosses to the desk, to above* ROGER.)

ROGER. I expect Miss Gwynne would like a taxi.

BEATRICE. Oh, no—I feel like walking. (*She comes to the front of the desk.*) Oh—I don't think you've got my private address. (*To* ELSIE.) I wonder if you'd mind taking it down?

(ELSIE *unwillingly does so.*)

Forty-four Glenster Grove House—it's just off Cheyne Walk. (*To* ROGER.) I always think forty-four such a nice easy number to remember, don't you?

ROGER. Yes.

BEATRICE. Good-bye. Thank you for helping me. (*She moves* L.)

ROGER (*rising and crossing down* C. *to her*). We haven't got very far yet.

BEATRICE. I'm sure we shall get much further next time we meet. Good-bye. (*At last, she puts on her hat.*)

(ELSIE *stares at the flowers in it, outraged.*)

(*To* ELSIE, *sweetly.*) Good-bye.

(*She goes out.*)

ELSIE. Well! (*She looks with wrath at the bowl of scillas.*)

ROGER (*crossing back and sitting at the desk*). I'm sorry. I couldn't stop her.

ELSIE. Fancy walking into anyone's office and grabbing the first thing that takes your fancy.

ROGER (*running through the letter*). Very reprehensible character.

ELSIE (*still considering* BEATRICE). Well, I must say!

ROGER (*signing the letter and handing it to her*). There. Now run along and get some air.

ELSIE. But you said——

ROGER. Oh, Lord—I was going to drive you home, wasn't I ? (*He rises.*) Look here—get yourself a taxi out of the petty cash, will you ? (*Crossing* L.) I've got to get home early—something I'd forgotten. An appointment.

ELSIE. An appointment ? Oh, I see—for this evening.

ROGER. Yes. An appointment for this evening. Good night. Get yourself that taxi.

(*He goes out, in very high spirits.* ELSIE *looks after him, disconsolate.*)

CURTAIN.

ACT III
Scene 1

Scene.—*The back garden of the* Hiltons' *House.* 6.45 *p.m.*
It is early twilight; there is a pearly quality in the light and sky. On the R. *is the house, the kitchen door and window on the ground level. An iron staircase ascends above them to a balcony which is outside the windows of a sitting-room. A wall runs across the back of the stage, beyond which is a vista of houses and trees. A few daffodils are growing round a tree* L., *but there are no beds or attempts at a formal garden.*
(*See Photograph of Scene.*)

When the Curtain *rises,* Martin Hilton *and* Alistair Brown *are seated in two deck chairs in the* C. *of the stage;* Martin L., Alistair R. Alistair *is twenty, fair, with regular features and a charming manner. He is lying back in his chair, looking at the sky.* Martin *is absorbed in a motor catalogue, taken from a pile at his side. One or two weighty-looking text-books lie discarded on the grass. Several very modern books and magazines are beside* Alistair.

Martin. You know, Alistair, that's an awfully snappy little bus.
Alistair (*amused*). Is it? Let's have a look at it.

(Martin *hands the catalogue.*)

I'm afraid that's a bit skittish for Mother. If we're getting a powerful car, it'll have to be one with a really roomy back with footstools and a table and a little vase of flowers.
Martin. Whatever for?
Alistair. To distract Mother's attention from the speedometer. —Don't let's talk about cars any more. I've been thinking a lot about you, lately, Martin.
Martin. Have you? Why?
Alistair. Just trying to make up my mind about you.
Martin. What on earth are you talking about?
Alistair (*after a moment's silence*). Martin, have you enough guts to chuck going into your father's business?
Martin. Good Lord, I've never thought about it. I've got to go into something.
Alistair. But isn't there something you'd really like to do?
Martin. Oh, I dunno. I'd like to have something to do with cars, of course.

ALISTAIR (*smiling*). You'll grow out of that—once we get one you can drive yourself.—I say, are you desperately keen on a very sporting car?

MARTIN. Well, of course I am. But it's your mother's car. She'll have to have what she likes.

ALISTAIR. I wonder. We'll see, my child. (*He relapses into silence, gazing at the sky.*)

MARTIN. You are the most extraordinary chap. Have you really been spending days wondering if I ought to go into Dad's office?

ALISTAIR. Not that entirely. You see, I've got to take up something too. Do you think you could be interested in interior decoration?

MARTIN. What, house-painting?

ALISTAIR. Well, more or less. Designing people's rooms—working out colour schemes—finding lovely things to sell.

MARTIN. I wouldn't be any good at that sort of thing.

ALISTAIR. I'm not so sure. And anyhow—I'd look after that side. I'd just want someone for the business part.

MARTIN. Do you mean, you'd start a business?

ALISTAIR. Yes. Mother'd stump up the capital.

MARTIN. But look here, do you think you ought to choose me? I'm no good at artistic things.

ALISTAIR. You're very quick at picking things up. Besides, I tell you—I'd do all that. All that matters is that we should really get on.

MARTIN. We do that all right. I say—it's jolly queer when you come to think of it.

ALISTAIR. What is?

MARTIN. That we do get on. We've hardly a thing in common. You're so frightfully brainy—not a bit like any of the chaps I've ever been friends with.

ALISTAIR. Brains have got very little to do with friendship. (*Suddenly.*) Martin! Are you terribly keen on driving at Easter?

MARTIN. Why?

ALISTAIR. Well, if we want to talk about this thing——. How would you like to walk?

MARTIN. What—just hike?

ALISTAIR. If you must call it that. We could try the Cotswolds.

MARTIN. I did rather fancy driving.

ALISTAIR. Oh well, if you want to. But this is jolly important.

MARTIN. Yes—all right.

(*The sound of a piano being played in the house is heard. The piece is Henselt's " Si Oiseau j'étais."*)

ALISTAIR. Who's that playing?

MARTIN. Ann—it's her concert piece. We get it morning, noon and night.

(*For a moment they listen in silence.*)

ALISTAIR. Queer how some moments crystallize themselves for one. I believe when I'm an old man I shall remember this garden and that tune.

MARTIN. What a funny thing to say.

(*They listen a few seconds. The music breaks off.*)

ALISTAIR. She's stopped. I'm going. Would you like to come out to-night? There's a marvellous film at the Curzon. (*He is collecting his books, etc.*)

MARTIN. The Curzon's a bit expensive, isn't it?

ALISTAIR. This is my party. And, Martin, if your parents are huffy about Easter you can count on me for expenses. Then you can snap your fingers at them.

MARTIN. But I couldn't possibly let you——

ALISTAIR (*rising*). Nonsense.

MARTIN. I'll tell you what—I'll borrow it and pay you back. I shall get a salary when I go into Father's office.

ALISTAIR. And supposing you don't go into your father's office?

MARTIN (*sitting up*). Oh, good Lord—do you mean you might start this scheme at once?

ALISTAIR. I don't know. We'll settle it at Easter. Good-bye, Martin. (*He ascends the stairs to the balcony.*) Nine o'clock outside the Curzon. I'll book the seats.

MARTIN. Thanks most awfully. And thanks about Easter, too.

ALISTAIR. I think Easter's going to be rather fun.—Good-bye for now.

(*He goes in through the sitting-room window.* MARTIN *stretches, whistling the melody of* "*Si Oiseau j'étais.*" *Then he picks up one of his text-books, opens and shuts it ruminatively, finally discarding it in favour of a car catalogue. After he has been studying it for a few seconds the head and shoulders of* JOAN COLLETT, *eighteen and enchantingly pretty, appears over the garden wall.*)

JOAN. Hi!

MARTIN (*startled and jumping up*). I beg your pardon. (*Crossing to the wall.*) I—have you lost a tennis ball or something?

JOAN. Of course not. We haven't got a tennis court.

MARTIN. No, of course you haven't.

JOAN. I did mean to come round to the front door, but I heard voices. Though it's really your father I wanted to see.

MARTIN. I'm afraid he's not back yet.

JOAN. It doesn't matter. You may be a bit more sensible than he is. (*She sits on the wall, her feet dangling on the far side.*) I think your father's an awful ass.

MARTIN. What on earth——

JOAN. It's that beastly dog of yours. He's always chasing our cat. And this morning your father was inciting him—positively inciting him.

MARTIN. I'm most frightfully sorry.

JOAN. I wouldn't mind as a rule, because cats can take care of themselves. But Silky's just going to have kittens.

MARTIN. Oh, good Lord!

JOAN. A shock might prove fatal.

MARTIN. Yes, of course. Is she going to have them soon?

JOAN. At any minute, I should think. I'm hoping she'll have them this week before Father gets back.

MARTIN. Why?

JOAN. Because she always manages to have them in his bedroom.

MARTIN. Why does she do that?

JOAN. We've never been able to find out.

MARTIN. Doesn't your father mind?

JOAN. He's not awfully keen. That's why I want her to have them while he's away. So if you could ask your father to see she isn't startled——

MARTIN. But I should have thought startling her would—well, I mean—— (*He gets suddenly embarrassed.*) Of course I'll speak to Father.

JOAN. It may not do much good. He looks very irresponsible. It must be funny having a parent like that. Mine are both elderly —and fat and tractable.

MARTIN. Are they? Funny, I haven't seen them yet. If they're elderly I suppose that isn't their Singer sports that stands outside your house sometimes.?

JOAN. Oh, that's mine.

MARTIN. Good Lord!

JOAN. Father gave it to me.

MARTIN. How perfectly marvellous.

JOAN. I suppose it is in a way. And yet, you know, life can be very ironic.

MARTIN. How do you mean?

JOAN. Now I've got it, I don't really like driving it. It's almost unbelievable, isn't it?

MARTIN (*fervently*). Quite unbelievable.

JOAN. You have to concentrate so hard. And you can't look at things.

MARTIN. Good Lord! I say—I mean, don't think it's the most frightful cheek, but—well, if you really feel like that——

JOAN. Do you drive a car?

MARTIN. Well, I drive our glossy new perambulator. As a matter of fact I did once drive a Singer sports.

JOAN. Would you like to try mine?

MARTIN. Well, of course I would. Wouldn't your people mind?

JOAN. Heavens, no!

MARTIN. I say, do come down this side, won't you ? I'll find a ladder.
JOAN. I can manage if you give me a hand.
·(*He helps her and she jumps.*)
Goodness, that was further than I thought. (*She moves down and flops into the deck-chair* L.C.) I say, who was that frightfully good-looking boy sitting here with you just now ?
MARTIN (*standing behind chair* R.C.). Alistair Brown. He's my best friend. Would you like to meet him ?
JOAN. I don't think so. I'm not keen on handsome men. There's always a catch about them.
MARTIN (*sitting on the* L. *arm of the chair* R.C.). Alistair's a marvellous chap. Frightfully brainy. I should think girls would find him fascinating.
JOAN. I shouldn't.—What are your sisters' names ?
MARTIN. Catherine and Ann.
JOAN. Is Catherine the eldest ?
MARTIN. Yes.
JOAN. But I should think she's a bit haughty.
MARTIN. She's got a foul temper.
JOAN. I'll tell you something. I've been wanting to know you all most awfully.
MARTIN. Have you really ?
JOAN. This is the first time we've lived in London. We don't seem to know anyone.
MARTIN. How rotten for you.
JOAN. I've been kicking about by myself all this lovely day. And just now, when I heard voices—well, I thought I'd pop over. Your dog chasing Silky was—well, a bit of an excuse. Do you think I'm awfully pushing ?
MARTIN. Rather not.
JOAN. We used to have such loads of friends up North. It feels all wrong down here. I wonder if Cath would be too haughty to come to tea.
MARTIN. I'll jolly well see she isn't.
JOAN. I thought she looked awfully interesting when she was sitting at the bathroom window this morning.
MARTIN. Oh, good Lord—I say, when I was shouting at her—you didn't really think I was——
JOAN. Shouting at me ? Just for a minute. But I soon saw. I was jolly disappointed, because I was going to shout back, and then we'd have known each other.
MARTIN. Well, we know each other now.

(*They smile at each other. Within the house* ANN *resumes her playing of* " *Si Oiseau j'étais.*")

JOAN. Who's that playing ?

MARTIN. Ann.
JOAN. She plays jolly well. That thing's awfully difficult.
MARTIN. Do you know it?
JOAN. I spent a whole term on it. It's called "If I were a bird."
MARTIN. Is it?
JOAN (*quoting in a rather flowery manner*). " Si oiseau j'étais à toi je volerais."
MARTIN (*grinning*). Is that French?
JOAN (*laughing*). Sh'rrup.—Do you know, that's a lucky tune to me?
MARTIN. Really?
JOAN. I learnt it my last term, when everything was lovely. Not one single thing went wrong. The Head said I was a reformed character.—That's why father gave me the car.
MARTIN. I should jolly well say it was a lucky tune.—I say, when would you like me to try driving it?
JOAN. To-morrow, if you like. (*Rising.*) I ought to go. We're going to the theatre to-night.
MARTIN. Which one?
JOAN. The new Cochran show. It's about all we haven't seen. We just go to the theatre because there's nothing else to do. We've been to thirty theatres since we came to London.
MARTIN. How marvellous.
JOAN. Heavens—I've just thought. Would you like to come?
MARTIN. Me?
JOAN. Because we've got an extra seat. Mother's so jolly absent-minded she forgot Father would be away.
MARTIN. Do you mean you were going to waste it?
JOAN. We don't know anyone to give it to. Are you doing anything?
MARTIN. Well—I was going to the pictures with Alistair.
JOAN (*sarcastically*). Oh! don't let's put Alistair out. Perhaps one of your sisters would like to come.
MARTIN (*rising from the arm*). They won't jolly well get the chance. I'll ring Alistair up.
JOAN. Good. (*Going up to the wall.*) I'll just pop over and tell Mother.
MARTIN (*going up* R.). I'll get you this box.
JOAN. It's all right—I'll go here. (*She goes over by the stairs.*)
MARTIN (*turning*, R.C.). I say, do I dress?
JOAN. I should think so. It's stalls.

(MARTIN *crosses to* L. *of the wall.* JOAN *is now sitting on the wall, facing* L., *and her legs dangling on the far side.*)

(*Turning her head to look up at the house.*) Do you know, I'm glad she's playing that tune. I shall remember it as long as I live.
MARTIN. Why?

Sc. 1.] CALL IT A DAY. 85

JOAN. I told you—it's lucky to me. Call for us at eight, will you—it's an eight-thirty show. (*She jumps down out of sight.*)
MARTIN. I say, are you sure your mother won't mind?
JOAN (*putting just her head over*). Mother's so jolly lonely she wouldn't mind if I brought the dustman home. See you later.
(*She disappears.* MARTIN *gives a sigh of signifying pleasure and the onset of tremendous activity. He looks at his wrist-watch.* COOK *comes from the kitchen with potatoes in a bowl and a saucepan of clean water. She places the saucepan on the stool down* R. *and settles in the chair* L. *of the stool with the bowl on her lap.*)
MARTIN. What time's dinner?
COOK. Same as usual, Mr. Martin—half-past seven.
MARTIN. I'd better dress before it. Will you please see it's punctual.
COOK (*busy peeling potatoes*). Shouldn't wonder if it mightn't be a bit late to-night, Vera being new.
MARTIN. It simply can't be late. I've got to be out by eight.
(*He starts collecting his books, etc.*)
COOK. Fancy that young lady coming over the wall.
MARTIN. Oh—you saw her, did you?
COOK. That'll make for trouble, that will.
MARTIN. What on earth do you mean?
COOK. Always a mistake to know the next-doors. It'll be "Could you oblige me with a drain of milk?" before long.
MARTIN. Nonsense. They're frightfully well off.
COOK. You can be a millionaire and run out of milk. You mark my words. Your mother won't be pleased.
MARTIN. Why not?
COOK. They'll always be popping in and popping out. Your mother's not one to be popped in on.
MARTIN. Well, I can't stop talking here. I've got to dress.
(*He goes up the stairs.*)
COOK. You got a clean shirt?
MARTIN. Why shouldn't I have?
COOK. I don't seem to remember one in the laundry for a long time.
MARTIN (*panic-stricken*). Oh, good Lord!

(*He dashes up the stairs and in through the window.* COOK *continues with the potato-peeling, gently murmuring her usual anthem, " I'm for ever blowing bubbles."* VERA *enters from the* L., *a light coat over her black dress and apron.*)

VERA (L., *brightly*). I'm back.
COOK. My word, you have been a time. Did you get lost?
VERA (*pleased with the suggestion*). Yes. That's what it must have been.
COOK. Here—where's the dog?

VERA. I met the master and he's taken him for a run. (*Moving c.*) Here's the mint. (*She produces a parcel.*)
COOK. You'd better get in and chop it.
VERA. Ooh, let's have a breather. (*She flops into the deck-chair* R.C.) That Terry doesn't half pull on the leash. What do you think he did?
COOK. What?
VERA. He went after that bulldog.
COOK. Did they fight?
VERA. Oh, no, they were ever so friendly. Funny, I've never thought of a bulldog being a lady. The gentleman was ever so nice. Said it wouldn't hurt a hair of anyone's head. Fancy, they're the gentlest dogs to have with children. Course, it's true about their grip, but they don't often fight. It's like men that don't know their own strength.
COOK. You learnt a lot, haven't you?
VERA. I'm getting quite fond of Terry. I'll take him out again this evening.
COOK. You've about run him off his feet already—in and out all day.
VERA. It's nice, sitting here.
COOK. Well, you won't be able to sit there any more. Mr. Martin's got to know the " next-doors."
VERA. What's that got to do with it?
COOK. You never been in a place where they know the " next-doors"? Every time the missus is out they just keep an eye on things for her.
VERA. Well, I'm sure Mrs. Hilton wouldn't mind anyone getting a breath of fresh air. After all, we're human beings. I'd tell her straight if she spoke to me about it.

(CATHERINE *has come out through the window and is descending the steps.*)

CATHERINE. Hadn't you better be doing something, Vera?
VERA (*rising meekly*). Oh, all right, miss.

(*She goes into the kitchen.*)

CATHERINE (*sitting in deck-chair* R.C.). I hope dinner won't be late, Cook, I've got to go out. (*She closes her eyes.*)
COOK. I'll do my best, miss—but Vera's a bit behind. You got a headache, miss?
CATHERINE. Yes.
COOK. I expect it tires you, sitting for that portrait, doesn't it?
CATHERINE. No. I wish you'd stop talking.
COOK. I'm sorry, miss. I'll just put these potatoes on.

(*She gives an indignant* " Ha!" *and exits, kicking the door open before her. Alone,* CATHERINE *opens her eyes and stretches her* arms, her whole mood one of nervous excitement and impatience. ANN comes from the kitchen, a piece of cake in her hand.)

ANN. Cook says you've got a headache. Shall I get you some aspirin?
CATHERINE. No.
ANN. Why don't you lie down till dinner?
CATHERINE. Because I don't want to. I haven't really got a headache. I just wanted to get rid of Cook. What time do you make it?
ANN (looking at her wrist-watch). Five past seven.
(CATHERINE flings herself back in her chair impatiently.) Are you going out to-night?
CATHERINE. Just for a walk.
ANN. I'd rather like to come with you.
CATHERINE (rising and crossing L.). Well, you can't.
ANN (moving to C.). Are you meeting someone?
CATHERINE (alarmed). What do you mean?
ANN. "What I said. "Are you meeting someone?"
CATHERINE (up stage L.C.). Of course not. But I like to walk alone.
ANN (sitting in the chair L.C.). I wish Mum would let me walk alone at night. I feel I could walk for miles. Funny, whenever I'm excited I get terribly hungry. (She eats her cake.)
CATHERINE (moving behind ANN to C.). What have you to be excited about?
ANN. My picture, of course. I think this is the most marvellous day of my whole life. Cath, I do think Mr. Francis is a wonderful man. Don't you?
CATHERINE. He's all right.
ANN. Mrs. Francis is nice, too—though she's not a bit the sort of person you'd expect him to marry. But I expect she understands him.
CATHERINE (moving R.C.). Oh, do shut up!
ANN. Why? If you haven't really got a headache——
CATHERINE (sitting in the deck-chair R.C.). Because I want to be quiet.
ANN. You're anything but quiet yourself. You never stop fidgeting. I should think you'd end by having St. Vitus's dance.
CATHERINE (sitting up). Oh, shut up, shut up. (She rises.) There's no peace anywhere in this house. I'm going to have a bath.
ANN. You can't, Martin's in.
CATHERINE. Of all the beastly, selfish——

(DOROTHY appears on the balcony. CATHERINE sees her and walks swiftly into the kitchen.)

ANN. Hello, darling. (She gets up and goes to meet her mother.)

DOROTHY (*coming down the stairs*). Hello, my pet. (*She kisses* ANN.)

ANN (*hanging on to her*). I'm sorry I was cross this morning.

DOROTHY (*at the foot of the stairs*). Were you cross?

ANN (L. *of* DOROTHY). Of course I was. Didn't you notice it? I stalked out in anger.

DOROTHY. So you did. And now Cath's stalked out in anger. What's the matter with her?

ANN. Just the glumps as usual. (*Pulling* DOROTHY *down stage.*) Come and sit down.

DOROTHY. Well, just for a minute. I'm rather tired. (*She sits in the deck-chair* R.C.)

ANN (*kneeling* L. *of* DOROTHY). Did you have a nice day?

DOROTHY. Pretty fair. I got you a new belt for your white linen. Do you want to see it?

ANN. Not just yet.—How was the matinée?

DOROTHY. Rather a morbid sort of a play. There was a clever girl in it.

ANN. Really?—Did you have tea at Fuller's?

DOROTHY. No. With Muriel's brother in his rooms.

ANN. Is he nice?

DOROTHY (*rather self-conscious*). Yes—quite. As a matter of fact he's coming here this evening. You'll have to do your lessons in the dining-room.

ANN. Oh, Mum—I can't. The beastly gas-fire makes popping noises and puts me off.

DOROTHY. You'll have to manage for once.

ANN (*heaving a giant sigh*). Oh dear.—I'm glad you had a nice day.

DOROTHY. Thank you. (*She sits back and closes her eyes.*)

ANN. You haven't asked me what sort of a day I had.

DOROTHY. Haven't I? Let's see. How was the algebra?

ANN. Foul. But it doesn't matter—nothing really matters. Mum, something terribly exciting's happened. (*She sees* DOROTHY'S *closed eyes.*) Mum, you're not taking an interest.

DOROTHY (*bestirring herself*). Yes, I am. What was it?

ANN. Well, I saw a picture and I didn't have enough money so I went for Cath and before I could borrow it they gave me tea and we talked and Mr. Francis found I was crazy about Rossetti and he gave me a sketch—not a print—a real, original sketch.

DOROTHY. Mr. Francis gave you one of his sketches?

ANN. Not his—at least, it was his but he hadn't done it. Rossetti had. He knew his father—I mean Rossetti did. And—oh, Mummy, I can keep it, can't I?

DOROTHY. Is it very valuable?

ANN. Only to me. At least—well, it may be a little bit valuable. But they promised me you wouldn't mind.

DOROTHY. Oh, well, I can't very well be ungracious to them. It's terribly kind of them.
ANN. Then it's all right?
DOROTHY. Yes, I suppose so.
ANN. Phew! That was easier than I expected. You must be jolly tired. (*After a pause, in a small voice.*) There's something else I've got to tell you.
DOROTHY. Yes?
ANN. I had to get the picture home and I'd a lot of school books. I was terribly frightened of damaging it so—I took a taxi.
DOROTHY. Did you have enough money for it?
ANN. I was going to borrow from Cath, but she had to go back for something and there I was.
DOROTHY. What did you do?
ANN. I borrowed from Cook—because the lock of my money-box got stuck.
DOROTHY. I see.
ANN. But, Mummy—aren't you angry?
DOROTHY. Because you borrowed from Cook?
ANN. No. Because I took a taxi. You told me I mustn't this morning. Only this wasn't a bit the same—and I was in it before I remembered. You know, when one's excited one does things one's not quite responsible for, doesn't one?
DOROTHY. Yes, I think perhaps one does.
ANN. And then you have to go on with them.
DOROTHY. Yes.
ANN. But I felt terribly guilty, I had to tell you. I'll pay Cook back just as soon as I can get that lock undone.
DOROTHY. You can tell her to put it down to housekeeping, if you like.
ANN. Oh, Mummy! (*She flings herself at her mother.*) I think you're the most understanding mother. Will you come and see the picture now?
DOROTHY. In a minute.
ANN (*rising*). I feel marvellous now. (*She sits in the deck-chair* L.C.) I don't think I'll ever feel any happier as long as I live.

(*They sit quietly for a moment. The light is fading.*)

Isn't it peaceful sitting here all friendly. What are you looking at —a star?
DOROTHY. Yes. There—just to the left of the chimney.
ANN. I see it. The first star's awfully lucky, you know. Isn't everything clear and pale. Shelley talks about the pale purple evening—but this isn't purple, is it? It's a sort of pearl. Wouldn't it be lovely to be a bird—only it would be an awful nuisance to have to flap your wings. I'd like just to float on a cloud. Do you think days know when they've been specially lovely and exciting things have happened on them? Do you think they feel pleased

with themselves? It's funny how some days are all grey and others are all shining. Isn't it nice us being all quiet together here?
DOROTHY. I wouldn't call you exactly quiet.
ANN. I'm quiet inside. (*Rising.*) Would you excuse me now? I'm just going to write a poem before dinner.

(*She runs in through the kitchen.* DOROTHY *sits quietly thinking for a second. Then* ROGER *comes out on the balcony, carrying a bunch of violets and an* "*Evening Standard.*")

ROGER. Hello.
DOROTHY. I didn't hear you put the car away.
ROGER. No. I've got to go out again.

(*He comes down the steps and drops the violets on* DOROTHY'S *knee. She looks a little surprised.*)

DOROTHY. To-night?
ROGER (*moving* L.). Yes. That girl—Miss Gwynne—her affairs are in an unholy muddle. I've got to straighten them out.
DOROTHY. Do you mean you're going back to the office?
ROGER (*down* L., *after a second's pause*). No—I'm going to see her. She was tired with the matinée to-day—she wasn't up to much. (*He feels self-conscious.*) By the way, you saw her, didn't you? Is she any good?
DOROTHY. Yes, she's rather remarkable. Queer and spasmodic, but full of feeling. Did you like her?
ROGER. Oh, so so. Yes, she seemed all right.
DOROTHY. Funny. I should have thought she was a girl one would have very definite opinions about. Must you go and see her to-night? Frank Haines is coming over.
ROGER (L.C.). Who's Frank Haines?
DOROTHY. You know who he is. Muriel's brother. We had tea with him to-day.
ROGER. What on earth made you ask him to-night?
DOROTHY. Well—he rather asked himself. I think he's lonely. Roger—— (*She stops.*)
ROGER. Yes?
DOROTHY. I'd like you to be in if you could.
ROGER. But I can't, I tell you. This girl's business is urgent.
DOROTHY. Surely to-morrow would——
ROGER (*up* C.). I can't put her off now—perhaps she can't manage to-morrow. She may be playing or rehearsing or something.
DOROTHY. I shouldn't think so. This was only a special matinée. Roger, I do particularly want you to be in.
ROGER (*moving down between the chairs*). My dear girl, isn't that damned unreasonable? This chap can't possibly want to meet me, and if he's anything like Muriel I shall be jolly glad to miss him.
DOROTHY. It's so odd you going out like this. You never have before. I can always count on you in the evenings.

Roger. Well, you counted on me once too often, didn't you, old lady ?—(*He kisses her on the top of the head and moves away to* R.) Look here, ring up and put Haines off till to-morrow.

Dorothy. No. I don't think I can do that.—Oh well, I suppose the children will be in.

(Martin *appears on the balcony, in his under-vest and black evening trousers. It is now late twilight.*)

Martin. I say, Dad, can you lend me a dress shirt ?

Roger. What for ?

Martin. To wear, of course. I'm going to the theatre—the new Cochran show.

Dorothy. Is Alistair taking you ?

Martin. No. (*In a whisper.*) I can't explain now. (*Coming down the steps.*) Can I have that shirt ?

Roger. What do you mean, you can't explain now ? What's the secret ?

Martin (*with frantic gestures indicating the next-door house*). I tell you, I can't shout it. (*The gestures continue.*)

Dorothy. What on earth does he mean ?

Roger. What's the matter with you ? (*At the wall.*) Is someone listening over there ?

Martin. Oh, for crying out loud ! (*Taking* Roger *down* L.) Don't you understand ? I'm going with the people next door. They asked me.

Dorothy. But we don't know them.

Martin (*crossing to* L. *of* Dorothy). Yes, we do. I mean, I do. The girl came over the wall——

Dorothy. I call that very pushing.

Martin. Oh, shut up, Mother. (*He looks nervously towards next door.*)

Dorothy (*not lowering her voice*). Do you mean she just came over the wall and asked you to the theatre ?

Martin. No. It wasn't anything like that. It's all to do with Dad really. You really must stop setting Terry after their cat. It's going to have kittens.

(Roger *gives a short amused laugh.*)

Dorothy (*to* Roger). Now you see what comes of your nonsensical behaviour this morning. I haven't the slightest desire to know these people.

Roger. Oh, Mother, do be quiet.

Dorothy. If you go out with them I shall have to call. You'd better ring up and say you find I'd fixed something up for you. As a matter of fact, I do want you to be in this evening.

Martin. Then I'm afraid you'll have to want, old darling. Can I have that shirt, Dad ?

Roger. Yes. Cut along and get it.

MARTIN. Thanks awfully. (*He suddenly puts his arm round his mother and gives her a quick hug.*) Terribly sorry, darling.

(*He runs up the stairs and off.*)

DOROTHY. Roger, you'd no right——

ROGER. Hey, hey, old lady—he's grown-up. You can't stop him making his own friends.

DOROTHY. You're always trying to stop his friendship with Alistair.

ROGER. Hm! (*Very pleased.*) Well, I'm not trying to stop his friendship with the young woman next door. She's damn pretty. (*He sits in the deck-chair* L.C., *then half rises.*) Good lord, I hope he's not taking one of my new shirts.

DOROTHY (*rising*). I'll see to it. I'm going up. (*She moves up stage, then turns on the steps.*) Roger.

ROGER. Yes?

DOROTHY. *Must* you go out to see this Gwynne girl to-night?

ROGER (*irritably*). Good Lord, Dot—what's the matter with you? Do you think I'm smitten with her or something?

DOROTHY. No. I hadn't thought of that. (*But she has now.*)

(*She looks speculatively at the flowers, then, with equal speculation, at* ROGER. *Then goes quietly up the stairs. Just before she enters the house, she looks back at him and gives a tiny snort, indicating irritation and surprise, but also a grain of amusement.* ROGER *looks up, but she goes quickly in.*)

ROGER (*conveying doubtful rumination*). Hm!

(*He picks up his paper, but it is too dark to read and he discards it irritably. He looks at his watch, gets up, sits down again, obviously on edge. There is very little daylight left. The kitchen door opens, letting out a flood of light.* MRS. MILSOM *comes out, ready for home, clutching a string bag and a curiously shaped newspaper parcel.*)

MRS. MILSOM (*speaking to* COOK *in the kitchen*). See you Monday, if I'm spared.

(*She moves across the garden. On seeing* ROGER *she gives a start and drops her parcel, out of which rolls an astounding collection of food, including an ancient cabbage, several apples and an old bone.*)

Oh, my word, sir—I didn't see you.

ROGER. I'm sorry.

MRS. MILSOM. It's my heart. It'll let me down one of these days. (*She starts to pick up the scattered food.*)

ROGER (*rising*). Let me give you a hand. (*He gets on his hands and knees.*)

(*Both their faces are lit by the shaft of light from the kitchen door.*)

MRS. MILSOM. Thank you, sir. Just a few things Cook had over. It was me or the dustbin.

Roger. You or the dustbin.
Mrs. Milsom. If I hadn't had them, they'd have gone in the dustbin. I don't like waste.
Roger (*crossing* R.). Quite right.
Mrs. Milsom (*retrieving the decrepit cabbage*). Course, they're not really fit for human consumption. But I thought they might do for my husband.
Roger (*returning a bruised apple*). That's the lot, I think.
Mrs. Milsom. Thank you, sir. Sorry to have troubled you.
Roger. Not at all. (*He sits in the deck-chair* R.C.) Pleasant day it's been.
Mrs. Milsom (*kneeling* C. *and doing up the parcel*). There's some'd call it that. I don't care for this sort of weather myself—boiling hot one minute and turning cold the next.
Roger. But has it been cold?
Mrs. Milsom. I'm not saying it has. But it might of. And the sunlight showing up every speck of dirt. I started my white paint this morning, but I couldn't finish it. My back wouldn't let me.
Roger. Sorry to hear that.
Mrs. Milsom (*finishing her paper parcel*). There. I expect it'll burst again before I get home. (*She struggles to her feet.*) My word, my back is bad and no mistake. And I'll have to finish that paint now I've started it. A day like this lets you in for things.

(Roger *gives a short laugh.* Ann *puts her head through the curtains.*)

Ann (*calling*). Daddy. Dinner.

(*She goes in, drawing the curtains.*)

Roger (*rising*). Early, isn't it?
Mrs. Milsom. Cook's been rushing it as you've all got fish to fry. Good night, sir.

(*She goes off* L.)

Roger. Good night.

(*The light behind the drawn sitting-room curtains goes on. A gong sounds within the house.* Roger *runs up the steps.*)

Curtain.

Scene 2

Scene.—*The bedroom shared by* Catherine *and* Ann. 11.30 *p.m. There is a door in the back wall and a window in the right.* Cathe-

RINE'S *bed is near the window*, ANN'S *bed runs down from the* L.C. *of the back wall.*

The furniture is simple, painted and rather childish. CATHE-RINE'S *part of the room is bare of pictures and books, except for a few magazines by her bed.* ANN'S *part of the room has several little bookcases, and the wall above her bed is crowded with pictures. These include several Rossetti reproductions and portraits of Rossetti, Browning, Shelley, Charles II, Napoleon and John Gielgud—the latter rather isolated, some distance from the bed. The Rossetti sketch is in the place of honour, over* ANN'S *head.*

When CURTAIN *rises, no details are visible, as the light comes only from a brilliant moon. The sound of stifled sobbing can be heard. Presently* CATHERINE *sits up in bed, searching for her handkerchief. She cannot find it and gets out of bed, still gasping with tears. She finds the handkerchief on the floor, looks warily at* ANN'S *bed and then goes to the window and gazes out. She slips to her knees on the bed, pressing her head against the pane. After a second,* ANN *sits up in bed.*

ANN. Cath—I'm not asleep.

CATHERINE (*turning*). Then you ought to be.

ANN. Oh, no I oughtn't. No one could sleep when you're going on like that. Cath, what's the matter?

CATHERINE. Oh, why can't you mind your own business? I might have known you'd be spying on me.

ANN. You don't have to spy to hear people howling.

CATHERINE. If only I could have a room to myself—just somewhere to crawl into.

ANN. I wonder if Mum would let me move into the attic?

CATHERINE. You know jolly well she wouldn't. We've just got to stick together and be two friendly little sisters.

ANN. Well, couldn't we be a bit friendly? I feel friendly, truly I do. Won't you talk to me?

CATHERINE (*burying herself in the bed-clothes*). Oh, leave me alone.

ANN. Perhaps it'll make it easier if I tell you I've guessed what's wrong. You're in love with Mr. Francis.

CATHERINE (*springing up in bed*). I'm not. How dare you say a thing like that.

ANN. Don't shout—they'll hear. It's no good, Cath—I'm sure. It came to me suddenly, this evening. I'm psychic, you know.

CATHERINE. You little idiot. It's not true, I tell you.

ANN. Yes it is. I don't blame you a bit. I'd be in love with him myself if you hadn't bagged him.

CATHERINE. Stop talking such utter nonsense. Don't you know he's a married man?

ANN. Well, of course I do. But that doesn't make any differ-

ence. People often fall in love with someone who's married. Lots of great people have done it. Perhaps you're going to be great, though I can't think what at. He likes you awfully, doesn't he?
CATHERINE. Did you think that?
ANN. Wait a minute. I'll come over.

(ANN *wraps the eiderdown round herself and crosses to sit on* CATHERINE'S *bed. Their faces glimmer white in the moonlight.*)

I think it's terribly romantic.
CATHERINE (L. *on her bed*). Aren't you shocked?
ANN (R. *on* CATHERINE'S *bed*). You can't shock a person whose favourite king is Charles the Second. Do you want him to leave his wife and marry you?
CATHERINE. I don't know what I want.
ANN. I don't think he will. Lots of famous men have had quiet little wives like that. You'll have to be just an inspiration to him.
CATHERINE. Oh, you don't understand. You think it's just hero-worship like you have for your poets and kings.
ANN. No, I don't—not now I've seen him. I expect you'd like him to kiss you, wouldn't you? Has he ever?
CATHERINE. No. He nearly did once. Do you remember the first time I went out early?
ANN. About three weeks ago?
CATHERINE. Yes. I went up on to Primrose Hill to think and —it was like a miracle, he was there.
ANN. How marvellous.
CATHERINE. It was all sort of misty—and then the sun came out. He said the most wonderful things. I know he was going to kiss me.
ANN. Why didn't he?
CATHERINE. A beastly old tramp came along.
ANN. What a frightful swizz. Oh, Cath, what a pity it is you don't write poetry. It would be such a help to you. Would you like me to do a poem about Primrose Hill?
CATHERINE. No. It's got nothing to do with you.
ANN. Of course, I do see that. But I could have done a lovely poem. Have you been meeting him every morning when you went out early?
CATHERINE. No—never again. Something went wrong. The next time I met him he was quite different. He's been beastly to me, Ann—fighting me all the time.
ANN. That's his conscience.
CATHERINE. Oh, it must be, mustn't it? I was sure it was to-day. He promised to meet me to-night.
ANN. Oh, Cath! What happened?
CATHERINE. He never came. (*She is working herself up.*) I waited and waited. People stared at me. Oh, Ann, it was awful. I waited nearly two hours.

ANN. Oh, Cath—how dreadful. Perhaps something stopped him. Did you ring up when you got back?

CATHERINE. How can I ring up? His wife knows about it.

ANN. Well, in that case, I shouldn't think it would matter if you rang up.

CATHERINE. Oh, you don't understand. I don't even know if he cares for me. There have been lots of other girls.

ANN. Great men are often like that.

CATHERINE. It's just like something out of a book to you. I'll die if I go on feeling like this. Hour after hour, waiting. Oh, what am I to do, what *am* I to do?

(DOROTHY *enters up* C., *in nightdress and dressing-gown.*)

DOROTHY. What on earth are you children chattering about at this time of night? (*Her hand fumbles for the electric light switch.*)

ANN (*springing up*). Oh, Mum, don't put the light on—you'll spoil everything. We're looking at the moon.

DOROTHY. You ought to have been asleep for hours.

ANN. I have been asleep. (*Getting between* DOROTHY *and* CATHERINE.) Look, Mummy, isn't it a marvellous moon?

DOROTHY (*crossing with* ANN *and looking out*). It *is* lovely, isn't it?

(*Behind* DOROTHY'S *back* CATHERINE *is quickly mopping her eyes.*)

ANN. I thought you'd appreciate it.

DOROTHY. But you really must go to sleep now. Come along now. (*She shepherds* ANN *back to bed, talking while she tucks her in.*) Why didn't you come in to see Mr. Haines, when you'd finished your lessons?

ANN. Oh, Mummy, I quite forgot. I got so thrilled doing my composition homework.

DOROTHY. You might have looked in when you came back from your walk, Cath. Muriel's brother will think I've got no family at all.

CATHERINE. I was tired.

DOROTHY. You slipped off to bed without a word. There was a telephone message for you.

CATHERINE (*tensely*). Who from?

DOROTHY. Mrs. Francis. They're going abroad to-morrow—quite suddenly—joining friends in Majorca.

CATHERINE. But—but the picture isn't finished.

DOROTHY. She seemed doubtful if he'd ever finish it. I must say I thought it a bit casual after all those sittings. But artists are like that. (*She is still busy with* ANN's *bed.*)

(CATHERINE *gives an involuntary gasp.*)

(*Turning to* CATHERINE.) What, dear?

ANN (*springing up in bed*). Mummy, doesn't my Rossetti look

marvellous in the moonlight? Look—doesn't it? (*She stands up beside it.*)
DOROTHY. Oh, Ann—when I've just tucked you in! Lie down at once. Yes, it looks lovely.—I'll draw the curtains now.
ANN (*catching her hand, to keep her from* CATHERINE'S *side of the room*). Oh, no—please, Mummy.
DOROTHY. Well, promise not to go moon-gazing again.
ANN. I promise. Good night, darling.
DOROTHY. Good night. (*On her way to the door.*) Do you mind very much about the picture, Cath?
CATHERINE (*with an effort*). Oh, no—the sittings were rather a bore.
DOROTHY (*turning at the door*). We'll think of something for you to do, now they're off your mind. Heavens, that moon is strong. Now, no more talking.

(*She goes out, closing the door.* ANN *listens a minute, then dashes across to* CATHERINE, *who is choking with tears.*)

ANN (*kneeling at the head of* CATHERINE'S *bed*). Oh, Cath—don't—please. It's a frightful compliment really—he's gone away because of his conscience——
CATHERINE (*sobbing uncontrollably*). To leave me without a word —oh, if only I could die——
ANN. Cath—oh, please stop—they'll hear you. Here—(*she pulls the eiderdown up over* CATHERINE'S *head*) you cry under that.
CATHERINE. I haven't anything left—not even a letter from him. Nothing.
ANN. Oh, goodness, I wish I could help.

(*She suddenly runs and puts her bedside light on. The array of pictures is instantly visible, the Rossetti sketch in the place of honour,* C. *above the head of her bed. Quickly she takes it down.*)

(*Crossing* R. *again.*) Cath, would you like this? It belonged to him.
CATHERINE (*coming miserably from under the eiderdown*). What? Oh, that. I don't want it. He gave it to you.
ANN. But it's something he's touched. Please let me—well, lend it to you. I'd like to. Oh, good egg, there's a nail where the "Three Kittens" used to hang. (*She hangs the picture over* CATHERINE'S *bed.*) There—look. You can touch the frame in the night if you want to. (*Crossing* L.) I'll just put John Gielgud back.

(*She takes John Gielgud's photograph from off the bookcase up* L. *and restores it to its rightful place—that vacated by the Rossetti.*)

CATHERINE. Oh, what am I going to do?
ANN. He's bound to come back some time. And he'll want to finish that portrait. Great artists never let anything get in the way of their work.
CATHERINE. But to go off like that—to get his wife to ring up. I'd have been content with so little—just to see him sometimes.

ANN. I shouldn't think you would. Not for very long. (*She takes the "Oxford Book of Verse" from the shelf over her bed.*)
CATHERINE. What are you doing?
ANN. I want to read you something. It's not like ordinary poetry. I think it will help you to sleep.
CATHERINE. They'll hear you.
ANN (*putting her ear against the wall*). No they won't, they're busy talking. (*She finds her place.*) I'll read it by the moonlight. (*She turns her bedside light out and goes to the window, standing with her back to it.*) I promised not to look at the moon, but this isn't exactly looking at it. Listen. It's by Alice Meynell.

(*She reads in a simple school-girl way, without expression, but sweetly.* CATHERINE *listens apathetically at first; gradually becoming absorbed in the poem. The two girls are absolutely still in the cold moonlight.*)

* " I must not think of thee ; and, tired yet strong,
I shun the thought that lurks in all delight—
The thought of thee—and in the blue heaven's height,
And in the sweetest passage of a song.
Oh, just beyond the fairest thoughts that throng
This breast, the thought of thee waits hidden yet bright;
But it must never, never come in sight;
I must stop short of thee the whole day long.
But when night comes to close each difficult day,
When sleep gives pause to the long watch I keep,
And all my bonds I needs must loose apart,
Must doff my will as raiment laid away,—
With the first dream that comes with the first sleep
I run, I run, I am gather'd to thy heart."

(*As* ANN *finishes,* CATHERINE *buries her face in her hands.*)

Oh dear, it's made you feel worse. I never thought of that.

(*The sound of knocking on the wall is heard.*)

Gosh—they're knocking.
CATHERINE (*whispering*). Get back to bed. I'll die if Mother comes in again.

(ANN *leaves the book on the floor near* CATHERINE *and scuttles into bed.*)

ANN (*listening*). She's not coming. Wouldn't it be frightful if she found out? Cath, mustn't it be queer to be old like that and know nothing exciting can ever happen to you?
CATHERINE. It must be jolly peaceful. They haven't a worry in the world. (*She is trying to find the Meynell sonnet by moonlight.*)

* Reprinted by kind permission from "Selected Poems of Alice Meynell" published by The Nonesuch Press.

ANN. Cath, if my Rossetti isn't any *real* help to you, I think perhaps I'll have it back to-morrow.

(*The knocking is heard again.* CATHERINE *drops the book and covers herself up.* ANN *dives under the bed-clothes.*)

CURTAIN.

SCENE 3

SCENE.—DOROTHY *and* ROGER'S *Bedroom.* 11.45 *p.m.*

When the CURTAIN *rises, the room is empty. The door to the passage stands open.* ROGER *comes from the bathroom in pyjamas and dressing-gown. He picks up his watch from the bedside table and winds it, then takes a cigarette from his case, lights it and moves about slowly but restlessly, looking preoccupied. Finally he comes to anchor by the window.* DOROTHY *comes in* R. *closing the door after her.*

DOROTHY (*crossing* L.). Talking forty to the dozen at this time of night. (*She goes into the bathroom.*)

ROGER. What?

DOROTHY. The children were chattering. (*She returns, with a bottle of setting lotion.*) The moonlight's keeping them awake.

ROGER (*looking out of the window*). Can't see any moon.

DOROTHY. You can't expect it to be on two sides of the house at once.

(ROGER *wanders round in front of the dressing-table.*)

Do get out of the way, dear. I want to set my hair.

ROGER. Oh! Right! (*He crosses* R.)

DOROTHY (*sitting at the dressing-table, pressing her hair into waves*). I'm trying to make it last the week.

ROGER. What? Oh, yes.

DOROTHY. Cath doesn't seem at all upset about Francis leaving her portrait unfinished. I should have been frightfully hurt at her age.

ROGER (*sitting on the* R. *edge of the bed* R.C.). He'll finish it some time.

DOROTHY. One never knows with these erratic people. Fancy going off to Majorca like that.

ROGER. Knocks your little idea on the head, doesn't it?

DOROTHY. What idea?

ROGER. That he was making love to Cath.

DOROTHY. I never said any such thing. The idea only passed through my head. But I should have known if there'd been anything like that really—one can always tell. I wish Martin would come in.

G*

ROGER. He's probably gone out to supper.
DOROTHY. Oh, I do hope not. We know nothing about these next-door people.
ROGER. Don't be such a fat-head.
DOROTHY. What time is it?
ROGER. Ten to twelve. What's-his-name stayed pretty late.
DOROTHY. Muriel's brother? Did he? I didn't notice. I must say I think you might have come in for a minute instead of creeping upstairs.
ROGER. What's the use of coming in when a chap's just going? Anyhow, I didn't feel like it. Was he desperately boring?
DOROTHY. No. He wasn't at all boring.
ROGER. Good.
DOROTHY. How was your actress friend?
ROGER. Oh, all right. (*Changing the subject.*) Is that those children talking? (*He rises and moves* c.)
DOROTHY. Oh, good heavens—bang on the wall, will you?

(ROGER *goes up between the beds and bangs on the wall.*)

Did you get through all your business?
ROGER. Pretty well.—Is that Martin? (*He goes to the door* R. *and opens it.*)
DOROTHY. Well? Is it?
ROGER (*closing the door*). No. (*He wanders back* c.)
DOROTHY. Tell me about Beatrice Gwynne.
ROGER. Oh, good Lord—— (*He sits on the* L. *edge of the bed* R.C.)
DOROTHY (*turning*). What's the matter?
ROGER. Can't you let the girl drop?
DOROTHY. What on earth do you mean? I'm simply taking a normal interest in——
ROGER. Normal my foot. You've been one mass of suspicion ever since I first mentioned her.
DOROTHY. Well I'm damned! Of all the idiots. If you want to put thoughts into my mind——
ROGER. Can you honestly tell me you haven't had your teeth into Beatrice Gwynne since the first minute you knew I was going to see her?
DOROTHY. Certainly I can.
ROGER. Then you're not even a very good liar.
DOROTHY. Roger!—Look here, this is getting rather ridiculous, isn't it? Let's not shout. I'll be perfectly honest with you. I did think it was a bit queer when you absolutely refused to cancel your appointment with her——
ROGER (*satirically*). You did?
DOROTHY. But I wasn't suspicious—not really suspicious. I'm sorry if I gave you that impression.

Roger. Oh, don't apologize.

Dorothy. Though I'm damned if I know why you should get savage about it unless——

Roger. Unless there was something in it. Go on, say it.

Dorothy. Stop putting words into my mouth. What's the matter with you? I've told you I'm sorry if I seemed suspicious. I've never been suspicious before.

Roger. You've never had any cause before.

Dorothy. Then I have cause now? I see. Well, do you want to talk about it? If not, let's drop it. (*She turns back to the dressing-table and continues to set her hair.*)

Roger. I'm not a good hand at this sort of thing.

Dorothy. You'll improve with practice.

Roger (*rising*). We'd better have it out, hadn't we? (*He crosses towards the door* R.)

Dorothy (*busily shaking her setting lotion*). You can do exactly what you please.

Roger. For God's sake stop putting that filthy stuff on your hair.

Dorothy. It isn't filthy. Oh, damn—I've pushed the waves all wrong. (*Turning round to him.*) All right, let's have it out. I suppose you've been flirting with the girl. She's young enough to be your daughter, anyhow.

Roger. Yes. I know that.

Dorothy. But a man's as old as he feels, isn't he? And you felt jolly young.

Roger. I feel damn old now.

Dorothy (*suddenly quieter*). What happened? You want to tell me, don't you?

Roger (*crossing* c.). Good God, I believe I do. I've made an awful fool of myself, Dot.

Dorothy. Did she start it?

Roger. Yes. What made you think that?

Dorothy. I know her type.

Roger. I don't think she's a type. She's very unusual.

Dorothy. Because she made a dead set at you? Don't be such an idiot. All modern girls just grab what they want.

Roger. All?

Dorothy. Unless they've been properly brought up, like our children.—I suppose she found the office hampering to a flirtation, so she asked you to her flat.

Roger. Yes.—Dot, it wasn't a flirtation.

Dorothy. What do you mean? Roger! Do you mean you're in love with her?

Roger. Not exactly. But—it wasn't a flirtation. Not this evening.

Dorothy (*rising*). Roger! Oh, my God, you couldn't—the first time you met. Not even a girl like that could——

ROGER. She's not a girl like anything. She's outside ordinary limitation.
DOROTHY. How dare you. Oh, how utterly beastly. And you stand there justifying her——
ROGER. I'm not justifying anything. (*Moving* R. *and then back to* L.C.) Phew! I'm glad I don't go in for this sort of thing often. Just stop jumping to conclusions, will you?
DOROTHY (*thoroughly rattled*). Roger, will you tell me at once what happened?
ROGER. Nothing happened. But it wasn't a flirtation.
DOROTHY. Then what was it?
ROGER. I don't know. She's not a girl you can flirt with. There's something ruthless about her. I think she'll be a great actress one day.
DOROTHY. What on earth's that got to do with it? You say nothing happened——
ROGER. As a matter of fact Harold Fawcett turned up at about ten o'clock.
DOROTHY. And if he hadn't?
ROGER. I don't know.
DOROTHY (*returning to her hair savagely*). Well, you can find out. There'll be plenty of other evenings.
ROGER. Dot——
DOROTHY (*seated at the dressing-table*). Why are you telling me all this? Are you getting some sort of kick out of it?
ROGER. Oh, my God! I'm sorry. You asked me to tell you.
DOROTHY. You seemed to want to. I didn't know you were just wanting to justify yourself—just gloating over the whole thing. (*She combs her hair indignantly.*)
ROGER. Oh, hell—do I look as if I'm gloating? You're taking it all too seriously.
DOROTHY. I see. You just wanted me to pat you on the back. You'd like me to be the sort of wife who was amused at her husband having affairs—who had affairs herself. (*Turning round to him suddenly.*) Well, if you would——
ROGER. What the hell do you mean?
DOROTHY. If you want to know—I've had an offer too.
ROGER. A *what*?
DOROTHY. An offer. There's someone who—well, someone who——
ROGER (*bursting into laughter*). Great jumping Jehoshaphat—has this what's-his-name been holding your hand all evening?
DOROTHY. There's nothing whatever to laugh at. It's a very serious matter.
ROGER. Fell in love with you at first sight, I suppose.
DOROTHY. It was an accident.
ROGER (*laughing*). Ha!
DOROTHY. He mistook me for someone else. It's a long and very

sad story and I haven't the slightest intention of telling you about it.

ROGER. Thank you very much. Am I to understand that this —oh, what the hell is his name?

DOROTHY. Frank Haines.

ROGER. What a damn ridiculous name. Is this Haines proposing you should help him to enjoy his leave?

DOROTHY. It's nothing like that at all. He wants to marry me. The whole thing's on a different level from your beastly little intrigue.

ROGER. Oh quite, quite. Ever so high-minded. Just proposing to break up a man's home.

DOROTHY. He's not, I tell you. The whole thing's terribly sad. I sent him away——

ROGER. But you could whistle him back. Let me tell you, that if he ever sets foot in this house——

DOROTHY. He's setting foot in it next Saturday. He's coming to dinner. (*She removes her rings with dignity.*)

ROGER. My God, of all the outrageous women! What would you say if I asked Beatrice Gwynne here? What would anyone say of a man who brought his lady friend into the house——

DOROTHY. But Frank isn't my lady friend—I mean he's not my gentleman friend——

(ROGER *roars with laughter.*)

Oh, yes, you can laugh. I've done nothing I'm ashamed of. The thing's a tragedy for Frank, and I'm going to do everything I can to help him. I want him to meet the children.

ROGER. Well, for utter indecency, give me the high-minded.

DOROTHY (*jumping up and turning to him, still clutching the bottle of setting lotion*). I'm *not* indecent. (*In her rage she accidentally jerks the bottle.*)

ROGER (*clapping his hand over his eye*). Hell and damnation, that stuff's gone in my eye.

DOROTHY. Serve you right.

ROGER (*still holding his eye*). Oh, my Lord——

DOROTHY. Roger! Oh, good Heavens, what's in it? (*She looks at the bottle, alarmed.*) It can't really have done you any harm——

ROGER. Oh, no, I shall get to like it in time.

DOROTHY. I believe you're just trying to frighten me. Let me look——

ROGER. You keep away with that bottle.

DOROTHY. Let me—— (*In her anxiety to see his eye she again jerks the bottle.*)

ROGER. God in heaven—— (*He claps his hand over his other eye.*)

(MARTIN *enters* R., *in evening dress and smoking a cigarette.*)

MARTIN (R.). You two old darlings not asleep?

DOROTHY (*turning on him furiously and crossing* R.). How dare you come in without knocking!
MARTIN (*crossing* C.). I did knock. What's the matter? (*To* ROGER.) Has Mother just dotted you one?
ROGER. Just been throwing her hair tonic about.
DOROTHY. It's not a tonic—it's a setting lotion. (*She shuts the door* R.)
ROGER. It's all one to me. Don't fuss. I shall be able to get about with a stick and a dog. (*He is now recovered. To* MARTIN.) Had a good evening? (*He sits on the stool down* L.)
MARTIN. Marvellous, thanks. The old girl's a sport. I say, Ma, you will call on them, won't you?
DOROTHY. Certainly not. (*She sits on the* L. *edge of the bed* R.C.)
MARTIN. But, darling, you'll have to. I promised you would.
DOROTHY. Then you'd no right——
ROGER. Fight it out in the morning.
MARTIN. All right. You won't let me down, old lady, I know. Is this the lethal bottle? (*He looks at the setting lotion.*) Tut, tut, you ridiculous woman.

(DOROTHY *rises, takes* MARTIN'S *cigarette from his mouth and puts it in the ashtray which is on the table up* C. *She then returns and resumes her seat on the bed.*)

DOROTHY. Oh, get along with you.—Alistair rang up. He was waiting for you somewhere.
MARTIN (*crossing* R.). Great Scott. I forgot to put him off.
DOROTHY. Oh, Martin, how careless!
MARTIN. I'll ring him to-morrow. I've got to—about several things. Poor old Alistair. I'm afraid he'll be pretty sick. Oh, Dad—I thought you might like to know I shall be at home for Easter.
ROGER. Indeed.
MARTIN. I shall be driving Joan's car a good bit—but we'll link up for picnics. She wants to know us all. Good night to you.

(*He goes out* R.)

ROGER (*pleased about* MARTIN). Hm! (*Suddenly remembering.*) Where were we?

(DOROTHY *does not reply. She is sitting, near tears, with her head on her left hand, her right hand still clutching the setting lotion.* ROGER *rises and goes to her.*)

Dot!
DOROTHY. It's all so damn silly. You can do what you like about the Gwynne girl. I shall just call on the neighbours and preside over the family picnics.
ROGER. Oh, my dear.

(*He goes to her, sees she is still holding the setting lotion, and takes it firmly away. He crosses and puts it on the dressing-table, then returns and sits opposite her, on the* R. *edge of the bed* L.C.)

I don't want to do anything about the damn girl. I started by telling you I'd made a fool of myself.

DOROTHY. If you want to go on with it——

ROGER. Do you seriously think I should have told you about it if I'd been going on?

DOROTHY. You might. We do tell each other things. It's no use just forcing yourself to give her up.

ROGER. There's no forcing. I don't see myself looking the kind of fool old Fawcett looked. You know, it's queer, Dot, she *is* interesting and unusual—this afternoon I felt as if I must get to know her better. I could have sworn there was something to know. But—I knew everything essential about her in that first ten minutes.

DOROTHY. How do you mean?

ROGER. She'll never give anyone anything, unless it's through her art. One can watch that. (*There is a shade of wistfulness in his tone.*)

DOROTHY (*rising and crossing to the dressing-table*). Let's go to bed, shall we? I still feel a bit feminine and idiotic about her. (*She is putting on her little net bonnet.*)

ROGER. And how about your Frank Haines?

DOROTHY. That's different. I knew all the time he never really threatened you.

ROGER. And you think this girl really threatened you?

DOROTHY. I don't want to think about it. Is your eye better?

ROGER. Yes. Both of them.

DOROTHY (*crossing* R.). Are you ready for bed? (*She puts the main light out, leaving only the* R. *bedside light.*)

ROGER. You're a queer woman. Don't you want to have it all out?

DOROTHY. Some time perhaps. Not now. I just want to think. Is the window open?

(ROGER *rises and crosses to the window.*)

ROGER (*looking out as he sees the window is open*). Good Lord! There's that new girl of ours. She's got Terry out.

DOROTHY (*crossing* L.). At this time of night? (*She joins him at the window.*)

ROGER. She's talking to someone.

DOROTHY. It's that manservant at the corner house.

ROGER. Shall I shout? Terry's shivering. It's turned damned cold.

DOROTHY. She's coming now. Oh dear, I shall have to speak to her in the morning. I don't believe she'll do. (*She takes off her dressing-gown, puts it on the dressing-table stool, then goes to her bed and takes off her slippers. Then she gets into bed.*)

ROGER (*leaving the curtains undrawn and crossing* R.). I say. (*He sits on the* L. *edge of the bed* R.C.) Something's struck me. We've been married twenty years, haven't we ?

DOROTHY. Yes.

ROGER (*taking off his dressing-gown and slippers*). And this is the first time either of us has—how did you put it ?—had an offer.

DOROTHY. As far as I know.

ROGER (*rising, crossing* R. *and putting his dressing-gown on the armchair*). And we've both handed it to each other on a plate within ten minutes of being alone. (*Returning to between the beds.*) We shan't do very well as a dashing, modern couple. (*He sees that* DOROTHY *is lying back in bed, quietly crying.*) Hi, Dot.

DOROTHY. It's nothing. I'm just tired. I'll tell Frank I can't see him again. It'll be kinder in the end. I believe you'd have liked him.

ROGER. Like hell, I should. (*He gets into bed, throwing the eiderdown off.*)

DOROTHY. Those children are talking again. Thump, will you ?

(ROGER *thumps on the wall.*)

ROGER. Funny kids.

DOROTHY. Thank goodness we've made a happy life for them. They've no problems or difficulties. (*She suddenly sits up in bed.*) Roger, I've a feeling I *would* like to talk this out—to get it all straight between us.

ROGER. All right, old lady. We'll have it all out on the mat. But not now. Let's chuck it for to-night. All right ?

DOROTHY. All right.

(ROGER *turns the* R. *bedside light out, then lies down. There is a faint light from the window.*)

ROGER. Where's that damned eiderdown ?

DOROTHY. Funny, turning so cold after such a lovely day.

ROGER (*pulling the eiderdown on*). It was just a fluke. We shall be back to normal again to-morrow. Good night. (*He lies down.*)

DOROTHY. Good night.

(ROGER *suddenly stretches his hand across to* DOROTHY. *She takes it. He gives her hand a little squeeze and relinquishes it quickly. Outside, a clock begins to strike midnight.*)

CURTAIN.

FURNITURE PLOT

ACT I, Scene 1 and ACT III, Scene 3

Armchair down R.
Table up R. (against dressing-room backing).
Twin beds up C.
Standard lamps up R.C. and up L.C. (either side of beds).
Bed-table up C. (between twin beds).
White bathroom stool up L. (against bathroom backing).
Towel-rail up L. (on bathroom backing).
Dressing-table L.
Stool R. of dressing-table.
Stool down L.

ACT I
Scene 2

Electric cooker down R.
Dresser up R.
Easiwork up R.C.
Kitchen range up C.
Fender up C.
Mantelshelf up C.
Table C.
Armchair C. (above table).
2 chairs C. (either side of table).
Sink up L.
Window-shelf up L.

Scene 3

Armchair down R.
Sideboard R.C.
Dining-table C.
5 chairs C. (around table).
Hearth up L.C.
Mantelpiece up L.C.
Armchair down L.
Wastepaper-basket L.

ACT II
Scene 1

Chest on pedestal down R.
Settee down R.
Occasional table down R.C.
Mural bookcase up R.
Paint table up R.C.
Easel up C.
Long bench up C.
Rostrum down L.
Chair down L. (on rostrum).
Armchair up R.

CALL IT A DAY.

SCENE 2

Chair up R.
Corner cabinet up R.
Suitcase up R.
Bureau desk up C.
Chair up C.
Large vase of pampas grass up L.
Golf clubs and tennis racket up L.
Chest L.
Gun-case down L.
Sofa R.C.
Cakestand C.
Coffee-table down C.
Large armchair L.C.
Small low table L.C.

SCENE 3

Pedestal desk R
Armchair R.
Flat, faced with fake deed-boxes R.
Bookcase flats with fake books up R., up C. and up L.
Armchair C.
Single chair up L.

ACT III

SCENE 1

Stool down R.
Kitchen chair down R.
Deck-chair R.C.
Deck-chair L.C.
Stone pedestal of daffodils down L.
Stairs up C. (leading up to balcony).
Planted daffodils L.C. (in box round base of tree).
French windows up R. (on balcony).
Reverse of kitchen window R.
Potted ferns up R. (in box round balcony).

SCENE 2

Bed R.
Bed up L.C.
Bedside-table up R.C.
Bedside-table up L.C.
Pouffe L.C. (at foot of L.C. bed).
Bookcase up L.
Armchair down L.

PROPERTY PLOT

ACT I

Scene 1

Cushion and dressing-gown (ROGER) in armchair down R.
Book, ashtray and cigarette-box on table against dressing-room backing up R.
Bedclothes and eiderdowns on bed R.C. and bed L.C.
Bedroom slippers (ROGER) by bed R.C.
Bedroom slippers (DOROTHY) by bed L.C.
Water-jug and glass, vase of flowers and spectacles in case on table up C.
4 books, comb and mirror on shelf of table up C.
Handkerchief, watch and chain, wallet, keys, lighter, cigarette-case, pipe, pouch and card-case in drawer of table up C.
Bedjacket on bed L.C.
Hotwater-bottle in bed L.C.
2 towels on towel-rail on backing up L.
2 pairs and 1 single lace curtains and 2 pairs of green brocade curtains at windows L.
2 lamps, hand-mirror, glass tray, orange sticks, brush and comb, manicure set, powder-bowl and 2 scent-bottles on dressing-table L.
4 handkerchiefs and various cosmetics in drawer of dressing-table L.
Dressing-gown (DOROTHY) on dressing-table stool L.

Furnishings.
   Picture over bed.
   Light switch below door R.
   Light brown carpet.
   Glass finger-plates and handles.

Offstage Properties down R.
   Tray and pot of tea for two, 2 cups and saucers, sugar-basin, milk-jug, plate of bread and butter and "The Times" (VERA).

Offstage Properties up L.
   Shaving-mug and soap, razor-strop and razor and brush (ROGER).

Effects.
   Church chimes.

Scene 2

Saucepan, 2 toast-racks, toast and toaster on electric cooker down R.
Church almanack and electric switch above cooker down R.
Plates, dishes, cups and saucers, etc., cutlery basket, soup plates and slop basin on dresser R.
Coffee, sugar, sage and rice canisters, empty tin of Cadbury's cocoa, 6 large glass canisters, packet of salt, bisto and bread on platter in Easiwork R.C.
Packet of "Force," bottle of ink, boot polish, floor polish, dusters, etc., in bottom cupboard of Easiwork R.C.
Saucepan with 5 eggs in it, boiling kettle, service teapot, saucepan, frying-pan, teacloth on kitchen range up C.
Dish of bacon in oven of range up C.
Fireirons and dustpan and brush in fender in front of range up C.
Alarm clock, china figure and 2 canisters on mantelshelf up C.
Cow picture above mantelshelf up C.

Check cloth, kitchen tea-pot, tea-caddy and spoon, "Daily Sketch," 3 odd cups, saucers and teaspoons, bread and knife on plate, butter on plate, 3 plates, 3 knives and forks, bowl of castor sugar and spoon, pot of marmalade, pint bottle of milk, spoon and fork, and pencil stub on kitchen table c.
6 eggcups in holder, empty sugar-bowl and tongs, hot-water jug and milk-jug on tray on table c.
Cushion and back swab in armchair up c.
"Weet-Meet" in bowl, packet of "Weet-Meet" and soap in soap-dish on draining board of sink L.
Sink tidy, squeedge and dish-rag in sink L.
"Boxall," "Scourine" and soap powder on window-ledge L.
Blue check curtains on window L.
Peg and apron (MRS. MILSOM) on door down L.

Furnishings.
　White china door furniture.

Effects.
　Electric indicator over upstage door.

SCENE 3

Cushion in armchair down R.
2 pairs of blue curtains and pelmet and lace curtains at window R.
Runner, bowl of fruit, dish of prop. ham with slices of real ham, carving-knife, 2 glass candlesticks, 4 candles (in candlesticks), vase of prop. flowers, entrée dish and 6 blue plates on sideboard R.C.
Flower picture and pair of candle brackets over sideboard R.C.
Tablecloth, 5 napkins and rings, 5 cups, saucers and spoons—4 eggs in cups and spoons, teapot, hot-water, milk-jug, sugar-basin, 2 toast-racks, from Scene 2—5 knives and forks, 10 plates, butter in dish, wicker d'oyley, cruet, marmalade in pot, piece of marmaladed toast on DOROTHY's plate, cigarette-box, letters for ROGER, letters and catalogues for DOROTHY, motor magazines for MARTIN, green exercise book inside "The Motor," and torn wrappers on table c.
Crumpled "Times" in chair down c.
Clock, blue china figure, vase of prop. flowers, matches and ashtray and cigarette-box on mantelpiece up c.
Landscape picture and pair of candle brackets above mantelpiece up c.
Cushion in armchair down L.
Wastepaper basket down L.
Fireirons, gas-fire and fender in hearth up c.
Hearthrug up c., in front of hearth.
4 school books, pencil box and strap on hearthrug.
Picture on backing of door up R.C.

Furnishings.
　Fawn carpet.
　Bellpush L. of mantelpiece.
　Light switch above mantel.
　Bronze door furniture.

Personal Properties.
　Pipe and pouch (ROGER).
　Blue Pencil (MARTIN).

Offstage Properties L.
　Empty tray from Scene 2 (VERA).
　Hoover (MRS. MILSOM).

Effects.
　Church chimes.
　Electric doorbell.

ACT II

Scene 1

China vase on pedestal down R.
Cushion on settee down R.
20 miscellaneous books in bookcase up R. (top shelf).
25 miscellaneous books, 4 magazines and small chest in bookcase up R. (2nd shelf).
Small canvas, small vase, 12 odd magazines and special Rossetti picture in bookcase up R. (3rd shelf).
Bowl of turpentine, 3 paint-rags, jar of 12 paint-brushes, and palette knife on paint table up R.C.
Painting of Catherine and small turpentine container on easel up C.
Fair tapestry curtains at window up C.
Chair on rostrum down L.
Book and shawl (CATHERINE) on chair on rostrum.

Furnishings.
2 pictures on wall R.
1 picture on wall R.C. in window.
2 pictures on wall up R. (1 above each bookcase).
1 picture on wall L.C. in window.
1 picture on wall above door.
2 canvasses leaning against wall R.
3 canvasses leaning against wall L.C. in window.
4 pictures leaning against bookcase.
Pair of tapestry curtains surrounding throne rostrum.
Bronze door furniture.

Personal Properties.
Cigarettes, matches, money, paint-rag (PAUL).
Knitting (ETHEL).
Shawl (CATHERINE).

Scene 2

2 china ornaments, camera-case and field-glasses on corner cabinet up R.
10 china ornaments inside corner cabinet up R.
Leather hatbox on suitcase up R.
2 pairs of chintz curtains, with pelmet, and 2 single lace curtains at windows up L.C. and up R.C.
2 window-boxes with daffodils outside windows.
3 pewter challenge cups, a special picture and a large ashtray on bureau desk up C.
3 golf-balls, tobacco-jar, pouch and pipe, blotter, pen and inkwell, cigar-box, photo in frame, letters, papers, etc., in desk.
Shooting-stick by R. of desk.
China vase and mirror on chest L.
Green cushion and blue cushion on settee R.C.
Plate of cakes on cakestand C.
Lace cloth, 3 cups, saucers, spoons, basin of sugar, milk-jug and small plate on coffee-table C.

Furnishings.
Picture over door.
Picture above chair up R.
Picture above picture above chair up R.
Picture above cabinet up R.
Picture above desk up C.
Picture above picture over desk.
Picture above vase up L.

CALL IT A DAY.

Picture above chest L.
Picture above picture over chest.
Wilton runner carpet across front of stage.
Painted china door-furniture.
Light switch down R. of door.

Offstage Properties R.
Parcel of pink crêpe-de-chine and parcel of soap (DOROTHY).
4 miscellaneous parcels and parcel of deep red silk with bill inside (in carrier bag) (MURIEL).
Bouquet of almond blossom, teapot and cakebox of chocolate cakes (FRANK).

Personal Properties.
Handbag and powder puff (DOROTHY).

Effects.
Church chimes (St. James's, Piccadilly).

SCENE 3

House telephone, P.O. telephone, cigarette-box, matches, ashtray, bowl of blue scillas, brass inkstand and pen, glass tray of pens and pencils, 1 pencil (at upstage end), blotting-pad, sheet of blotting-paper, fountain-pen, spectacles and 3 files with letters for signing on desk R.
Various papers and Beatrice Gwynne income tax file in downstage drawer of desk.
Plain quarto paper in upstage drawer of desk.
Window-seats with long cushions and linen blinds in windows up L.C. and up R.C.
Special loose shutter-knob on window up L.C.

Furnishings.
Print above deed-boxes R.
Print above door L.
Brown carpet.
Certificate of accountancy between windows.
2 candle brackets: 1 R. of window R.C. and 1 L. of window L.C.
Light switch below door L.
Bronze latch handle on door L.

Offstage Properties L.
Notebook and pencil, letter for signature in folder, cup of tea (sugar in saucer) (ELSIE).

Effects.
House telephone buzzer in floats.

ACT III

SCENE 1

Tub and 2 folded deck-chairs under balcony.
Potted ferns on balcony.
2 textbooks and 2 motor magazines, in deck-chair L.C.
3 " arty " magazines in deck-chair R.C.
Beer box under stairs.
Blue pair of check curtains on reverse of kitchen window R.
1 pair of lace curtains at French windows on balcony.

Furnishings.
Flagged stage cloth.

Offstage Properties down R.
Potatoes in bowl of water, peeling-knife and saucepan of water (COOK).
Newspaper parcel of potatoes, carrots, cabbage, bread, bones and turnips (MRS. MILSOM.)
Slice of cake (ANN).

114 CALL IT A DAY.

Offstage Properties up R.
Bunch of violets and " Evening Standard " (ROGER).
Offstage Properties down L.
Dog's leash and bunch of mint (VERA).
Effects.
Piano playing Henselt's " Si Oiseau J'étais."
Gong.

SCENE 2

1 pair of blue net curtains and 1 pair of blue silk curtains and pelmet at window R.
Blue bedclothes and blue eiderdowns on beds R. and up L.C.
China lamp (dead), 3 books and 2 film magazines on bedside table up R.C.
China lamp (alive) and Temple edition of " Twelfth Night " on bedside table up L.C.
5 framed prints and special Rossetti from Act II, Scene 1, above bed up L.C.
Small wall bookcase with 2 prints on top shelf, small editions of Shakespeare on 2nd shelf and Oxford book of English Verse on wall L. of bed up L.C.
2 exercise books on pouffe L.C.
Framed picture of John Gielgud, bowl of flowers and 2 books on bookcase L. on top shelf.
50 miscellaneous books on bookcase L. on next three shelves.
6 boxes of children's games on bookcase L. on bottom shelf.
4 small framed prints above bookcase L.
Small wall cabinet with bowl of flowers on it above armchair L.
Furnishings.
All furniture painted blue.
China door-furniture.
Picture of landscape above CATHERINE'S bed.
Grey woolly rug C. of floor.

SCENE 3

See Act I, Scene 1.

Add ashtray to table up C.
Bottle of hair lotion off up L. (DOROTHY).
Cigarette off down R. (MARTIN).

DRESS PLOT
(as in London Production)

ACT I

SCENE 1

DOROTHY . . Light green nightdress, light green dressing-gown, light green woolly bed-jacket, light green mules.
ROGER . . (a) Blue-green silk pyjamas, black dressing-gown with green lapel facings, black bedroom slippers.
(b) Blue and white striped bath wrap.
(c) Grey lounge suit.
ANN . . . White satin nightdress, blue Jaegar dressing-gown, blue carpet slippers.
MARTIN . . Maroon poplin pyjamas, maroon dressing-gown, brown bedroom slippers.
CATHERINE . . Pink lace-trimmed "step-ins," peach velvet dressing-gown, peach mules.
VERA . . . Blue maid's outfit with white apron and cap.

SCENE 2

COOK . . . Pink flowered frock, white apron.
MRS. MILSOM . Black coat and skirt, 2 black-coloured cardigans, black coloured printed apron, small, thin, scraggy fur.
VERA . . As Scene 1.
ROGER . . As Scene 1 (c).

SCENE 3

ROGER . . As Scene 1 (c).
DOROTHY . . Blue-grey tweed coat and skirt, grey woollen shirt-blouse.
MARTIN . . Grey lounge suit.
ANN . . . Navy blue gym dress, white blouse, blue tweed overcoat with blue velour lapel facings, black velour school hat with plain blue band.
CATHERINE . . Beige tweed costume, brown woollen jumper, brown suède shoes.
VERA . . . As Scene 1.
MRS. MILSOM . As Scene 2.

ACT II

SCENE 1

PAUL FRANCIS . White painter's smock, grey flannel trousers, brown suède shoes.
ETHEL FRANCIS . Light brown skirt, green-coloured "arty" coatee.
CATHERINE . . (a) Wine-coloured model dress (tight waist and full skirt).
(b) As in Act I, Scene 3.
ANN . . . As in Act I, Scene 3.

CALL IT A DAY.

SCENE 2

DOROTHY	As in Act I, Scene 3. Carrying felt hat.
MURIEL WESTON	Black pin-stripe costume, white satin blouse, white hat.
FRANK HAINES	Blue-striped lounge suit, regimental tie.

SCENE 3

ROGER	As in Act I, Scene 1 (c).
ELSIE	Plain brown frock with white collar and cuffs.
BEATRICE GWYNNE	Red jumper-blouse, blue skirt, blue overcoat.

ACT III

SCENE 1

MARTIN	As in Act I, Scene 3. (a) Vest and dinner-jacket trousers.
ALISTAIR BROWN	Fawn sports jacket with pleats at the back, flannel trousers, brown suède shoes.
JOAN COLLETT	Light pink coat and skirt, light blue polo jumper.
COOK	As in Act I, Scene 2.
VERA	Brown maid's outfit, fawn lace cap and apron, navy coat.
CATHERINE	Light flowered silk frock.
ANN	Flowered crêpe frock.
DOROTHY	Deep blue semi-evening gown.
ROGER	As in Act I, Scene 1 (c).
MRS. MILSOM	As in Act I, Scene 2.

SCENE 2

CATHERINE	White satin lace-trimmed nightdress.
ANN	White satin nightdress.
DOROTHY	As in Act I, Scene 1.

SCENE 3

ROGER	As in Act I, Scene 1 (a).
DOROTHY	As in Act I, Scene 1.
MARTIN	Dinner-jacket.

Act I, Scene 1
and
Act III, Scene 3.

Act I, Scene 2.

[*Call It a Day*]   [*Photographs by the Stage Photo Co.*]

Act I, Scene 3.

Act II, Scene 1.

[*Photographs by the Stage Photo Co.*

Act II, Scene 2.

Act II, Scene 3.

[*Photographs by the Stage Photo Co.*

Act III, Scene 1.

Act III, Scene 2.

[*Photographs by the Stage Photo Co.*

www.ingramcontent.com/pod-product-compliance
Ingram Content Group UK Ltd.
Pitfield, Milton Keynes, MK11 3LW, UK
UKHW021842140426
5217IPUK00022B/1549